DISCARD

From
Here
To
There

Moving a Library

Dennis C. Tucker

 Wyndham Hall Press

FROM HERE TO THERE: MOVING A LIBRARY

by Dennis Tucker (University of Notre Dame)

Library of Congress Cataloging-in-Publication Data

Tucker, Dennis C.
  From here to there.

  Bibliography: p.
  Includes index.
  1. Library moving. I. Title.
Z703.5.T83 1987   025.8'1   87-28061
ISBN 0-55605-027-5
ISBN 0-55605-028-3 (pbk.)

TABLE OF CONTENTS

TO

Guillermina,

Andy, Billy, Eric, and Mike

iv   FROM HERE TO THERE

ACKNOWLEDGEMENTS

There are numerous people whom I must thank for their assistance and cooperation in the preparation of this manuscript. At the risk of forgetting someone whose help I received during the lengthy two-year process, I wish to thank these whose names come immediately to mind:

First of all, I must thank Mrs. Lola Mae Philippsen, director of Collection Development, and Sr. Bernice Hollenhorst, C.S.C., director of the Cushwa-Leighton Library of Saint Mary's College, Notre Dame, Indiana, without whose encouragement, advice and assistance I would not have survived my first move, and without whose constant smiles of approval I would never have undertaken this project.

My thanks to Margaret Porter of the reference department of the University of Notre Dame, whose expertise at computerized bibliographic retrieval saved me many days of letting my fingers do the walking through the weighty tomes of the professional literature of library science.

Thanks to Devon Yoder, library director of Goshen College in Goshen, Indiana, and to John Morgan of Bethel College, Mishawaka, Indiana, for their advice and listening ears when I needed them.

A special thanks to Mr. Wayne Woodworth and the late Harold (Rocky) Schuttrow of Woodworth Storage and Transfer Company, Allied Van Lines, South Bend, Indiana, who got me through my first move and gave me the confidence that I could do it again. Several of the ideas expounded herein, I owe to them. Thanks for their patience during my impatience and their wisdom in overcoming my ignorance. You are the best!

Thanks to Mary Ann Urbashich, reference librarian at the Area Library Services Authority (ALSA 2) in Mishawaka, Indiana, who turned the world upside down to find copies of obscure articles that no one had.

Thanks to Steve Brown, library director of Cedarville College, Cedarville, Ohio, Bob Kaehr, library director of Huntington College, Huntington, Indiana, and Martha Stratton, coordinator of ALSA 2, Mishawaka, Indiana, for their willingness to share their research with me.

I must gratefully acknowledge the help of Laura Fuderer of the Collection Development Department and Esther Matteson of the Cataloging Department of the University of Notre Dame who spent hours poring over the manuscript correcting every misused verb, overused comma, and misplaced modifier. Their offers of help came at a time when I urgently needed a fresh pair of eyes to help pick out the flaws in the manuscript, grammatical and otherwise.

And thanks to dozens of ILL librarians scattered throughout the country who, totally unawares, shared their resources with me through our marvelous national ILL system, the OCLC network.

Finally, a special thanks goes to my family who forwent numerous outings and days in the park. They often went quietly (and more often, not so quietly) to bed in the evening and just let me be, so I was able to get some work done on the manuscript.

D. T.

PREFACE

An old saying suggests that "three moves are equivalent to one good fire." Anyone who has ever moved a library collection can relate to that. One move can clean out a collection--fortunately, not as drastically as a fire would. Nevertheless, one move can produce as many headaches as a good fire for the librarian who has not had the advantage of experience: personal or reported by others. Dennis Tucker has gone a long way toward helping library movers avoid headaches, to say the least.

Before a move takes place, a lot of planning has to be done. There needs to be consideration given to the collection itself and its condition. When a move is in the offing, it is a good time to examine the condition of the collection, do the weeding that has been put off, and make the book repairs that have been postponed. It is a good time to take preservation steps, too. All of these issues are presented in detail within the text of this book.

What is involved in the actual move of a library? Regardless of the number of volumes in the collection, library materials consist of numerous small packages which have to be put together in larger containers for moving. What kind of larger containers are needed? Tucker has examined boxes, trays, troughs, and booktrucks for their utility in a move. Library materials are of differing sizes, too. What size and shape of boxes, troughs or trucks will serve best?

For the actual transport of the collection from the old to the new location, decisions have to be made concerning carriers. A local moving company is only one option. One move that I remember contracted with a local mover but used off-duty firefighters (no pun intended) to provide the muscle. As Tucker points out, some libraries have employed the idea of the bucket brigade passing books from one person to the next. Others have tried using library users to check out all the books and bring them back to the new location. These methods are innovative and perhaps newsworthy, but not particularly practical. They leave too much to be done after the move to straighten up mistakes in shelving. In the ideal, there would probably be no need for shelf reading after the move. Every item would be taken from the shelf in the old building, placed in exactly the right place in the new building, and no interruption in service would be experienced. Ideals are goals to aim for; but they are usually unattainable in the real world. The best we can hope for in moving a library is to minimize the amount of "clean up" work that must be done after the move. Tucker examines these potential problem areas. He provides advice and suggestions for avoiding the leftovers.

Coming full circle back to the beginning, the best way to avoid problems with a move is to plan thoroughly before the move takes place. Needless to say, commercial movers, when used, will always need to be engaged in advance. It will also always be necessary to schedule the move far enough in advance to minimize upsets in service to library users. But there is a myriad of small details which can be overlooked and which can trip up even the smoothest move.

This planning process for a move is not unlike planning for any other activity. A thoroughly informed and well led committee is probably the best alternative. The work of this group should continue throughout the whole process, ending only after the final dedication of the new facility with all the collection safely in place. This final dedication is a good time to thank the planners for doing a good job. By that time, it will be quite evident whether they deserve it; and they will, if they have followed the advice in this book.

The librarian anticipating the move of even a portion of a library's collection is well advised in the pages of this book. Read it well and you'll reduce the potential for pain and trouble when it is your turn to pack up and move.

Edward P. Miller,Ph. D.
Graduate Library School
Tucson, Arizona
August, 1987

INTRODUCTION

For most of us librarians who are called on to move a library, it is a once-in-a-lifetime experience. It is not surprising, then, that we should approach the task with trepidation. Lacking first-hand experience, as most of us do, where can we turn for outside help? A search of the library literature will reveal that precious little has been written on the topic, save a few books which are no longer in print or the occasional journal article entitled "The Students at Sainte Susie's College Moved the Library by Forming a Human Book Chain on Their Lunch Hour." Most of the authors of such articles are proud of the record speed with which they moved their books but invariably neglect to mention that it took three months of shifting to restore some semblance of order to the collection.

The librarian planning a move should take advantage of every opportunity to speak with those who have already had the experience. He or she should canvass the local area to discover libraries which have moved. Most of those who have survived the ordeal are proud of the accomplishment and eager to talk about it. Often, they have kept notes of all their preparations which they are willing to share with a colleague who is soon to face his trial by fire. He should not hesitate to call upon those people for expertise and ask to borrow their collection of materials.

Contact the local or state network or the state library to find out who has moved recently or is planning a move. Search the professional literature for news of moves. Several of the professional journals give an annual report of libraries which have been built in the past year. A story of a new building, one nearing completion, or even a groundbreaking is a likely indication that a move is about to take place. A story of a dedication ceremony for a new facility usually means that there has been a recent move.

If you are fortunate enough to locate a move about to take place, volunteer your services--on moving day if no other time. Walking in line in the rain while carrying an armload of soggy books is an almost failsafe guarantee that you will plan your move better. Serving as a volunteer at the bottom of the hierarchy will teach you about communication with workers as no book nor explanation can. You will see good points to follow and pitfalls to avoid as you face your own move.

It is not the purpose of this work to report on every library that has ever been moved. Nor is its purpose to provide a highly-documented and exhaustive study of moving methods. Rather, we want to show a few methods that have been tried and proven, and to share a few things we have learned along the way, but primarily to raise some issues and bring forth ideas which may not yet have occurred to the librarian who is facing a move. We will strive to be practical rather than theoretical, down-to-earth rather than inspirational; moving, after all, is a dirty job, but somebody's gotta do it.

The secret for a successful move is found in the key word -- "planning." In a nutshell, the key to moving all or part of a collection successfully, with a minimum of effort and confusion, is to plan carefully each individual element of the move, as far in advance as possible.

The planning for the move should begin long before the architect is commissioned to come up with a drawing. Moving and building planning are inseparable, as both are indispensable to the success of the final product --that product being, of course, service to the patron. It is only with careful planning that we can avoid such pitfalls as darkly lit aisles or running out of shelf space in a given area before we run out of collection. What can be done on moving day if there are no more shelves left in the Dewey 800 section and we have only shelved the collection up through the 870s? It is possible, of course, to shelve them at the end of the 500s, where there is plenty of space left over. But, how confusing will that make it for the patron to find a book? Planning the move in conjunction with the architect will help avoid such problems.

Or, supposing the move is all planned and on moving day we discover that the only door through which we can take the 900s into the new building has been blocked by the previously moved reference collection? Adequate planning would have shown us to move the 900s first.

When we get down to the nitty-gritty of the move, there are enough factors to be considered to give even the most stalwart among us a headache simply trying to remember them all: Who should be in charge of the move? When should the move take place? How should it be done? Should we do it ourselves? Should we hire a professional mover? How much will it cost? How long will it take? What should be moved first? Should we clean and fumigate the books as we move them? How long before the library will be open for service in the new facility?

In the following chapters, we will consider these questions and many others so that even the librarian who is faced with a first move can approach it with confidence and ability, and come away feeling satisfied after executing a successful move.

4   *FROM HERE TO THERE*

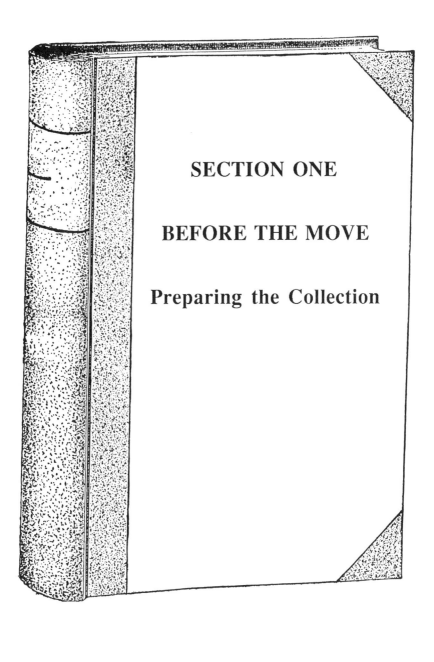

SECTION ONE

BEFORE THE MOVE

Preparing the Collection

6 *FROM HERE TO THERE*

CHAPTER 1

Appointing a Move Director and Establishing a Move Committee

The first, and perhaps the most far reaching, task in preparation for the move is the appointment of a move director. While the choice of a good move director will not, in itself, guarantee a successful move, the wrong choice will guarantee failure. Therefore, as the success of the move may hinge totally on this one decision, it should be made carefully and thoughtfully.

TIME FRAME

Planning for the move must begin very early. There are four steps to a move, each of which must be given plenty of time:

1) The selection committee needs time to make a wise choice for move director. The committee or person doing the selection of the move director will need to allow adequate time to consider all possible candidates, review the qualifications of each, and make an appropriate selection.

2) Depending upon prior experience, the move director may require considerable self-preparation before beginning to plan for the move. In many cases this move will be the move director's first, and he or she may need an extended period of time to prepare himself emotionally and scholastically to tackle a task of this magnitude. It is unfair to expect him to do a good job without giving him adequate lead time.

3) The planning process for a move is usually a long one. Before the move can even begin, it requires a long thought process. A lot of time must be spent simply brainstorming. What preparations must be made? How must the collection be gotten ready? What materials can be weeded? What furniture can be sold (or junked)? How long will this process take? What method should be used?

4) There must be sufficient time for the move itself. When is the best time for moving the collection? During a semester break in a college or school library? Or while students are still around to help with the move? Should the move be made on a weekend? At night? Or while trying to maintain regular hours? Let us suppose for a moment that the library has a deadline by which it must vacate its present location or occupy the new. How long will it take to move from location A to location B? Days? Weeks? Months?

The move director must be appointed in plenty of time for him to do his job. It may take weeks or even months of study on his part before he can formulate any kind of answer to the above questions. To press him into a time frame that rushes these decisions can only lead to tragedy.

QUALIFICATIONS AND RESPONSIBILITIES

What are the qualifications to look for in a move director? The first qualification is *time*. The move director must be someone with sufficient time on his hands to plan the move. He must be released from any and all conflicting responsibilities and demands on his time.

For this reason, it may not be wise to appoint the library director as move director. The library director is often caught up in administrative decisions which cannot be neglected nor postponed; to do so may harm library operations either presently or in the future. Yet, virtually no one but the library director himself can perform his administrative duties nor make decisions in his place.

On the other hand, a para-professional may be more easily released from regular duties in that it is easier to find and train a substitute to perform clerical duties. But a para-professional may not have a sufficient overview of library operations to be able to handle the job of moving. Often the duties of the move director include such tasks as planning which collections will be placed in which location in the new building or who will occupy which office. These are administrative decisions which are best made by a professional librarian, preferably a member of the administrative staff.

It is for these reasons, that a sub-administrator, such as an assistant director or assistant department head may make the best candidate. We must go far enough down the ladder of responsibility that the person chosen can be relieved of his or her normal duties without the necessity of shutting down operations and far enough up the ladder to find a person with some administrative experience and ability--a difficult combination to find. When moving their library, Utah State University decided to let the assistant librarian and the library department heads plan the move so that the librarian would be free to make decisions on other matters than the move.[1]

The move director must be able to turn concretes into abstracts and abstracts into concretes. He must be able to visualize what the new facility will be like when all the stacks are up and the books are on the shelves. He must be able to translate that vision to a piece of paper and then reconstruct it life-size during the actual move. He must be able to turn real books into an abstract number and bear in mind that the abstract number will have weight, bulk, and a tremendous mass on moving day.

The move director must have an understanding of statistics, sampling, and data-gathering techniques. He must consistently be able to produce an extremely high rate of accuracy in working with these figures. He must understand the various methods by which data can be gathered and realize that figures can often give a false reading. He must be able to control the figures to ensure their validity.

---

[1]Chappell, LaMont D. "Operation Move," *Utah Libraries* 7 (Spring 1964): 7-8.

The move director must be a good communicator with people at both ends of the ladder. He must communicate with superiors, and often present alternatives with his recommendation as to the most viable. Frequently he will be called upon to gain permission which others may be unwilling to give unless the situation is laid out for them clearly and accurately. There will always be a higher authority--the college president or dean, the chairman of the board of trustees, or the superintendent or principal--to whom rationales must be given at great lengths for each step of the process. If the director can win the confidence of that person, the task will be made much easier.

The move director must be able to communicate with those who will assist him, for these are the people who will do the actual sampling and data-gathering, as well as the physical moving. His communications must be accurate, clear, and concise to avoid any type of waste, as well as tactful enough to avoid misunderstandings and hurt feelings.

The move director must be able to locate and communicate with others who have had experience in moving, know how to interview them and glean their ideas. He must separate what works from what does not and understand why it does not. He must know how to apply what he has learned to the present situation.

The move director must communicate with patrons to keep them informed as to the progress of the move. These are the people who are bearing the brunt of the confusion and are often unable--or unwilling--to understand that the move is taking place primarily for their benefit. Others simply have a desire--and a right--to know what is going on.

The move director must know how to conduct research. A given for a librarian? Hopefully, but don't take it for granted. If the move director does not understand data-gathering techniques, he must know where to look or whom to talk to for more information. If he needs to find references for professional movers, or to locate a specific item of equipment, he must know where to look.

After conducting an extensive comparative study of library moves, John Kephart writes: "From a study of these 17 cases one generalization stands out pre-eminent. It is that the librarian who is planning to move must know his own situation thoroughly. This may seem to be self-evident, but the need of knowing one's own situation is so important that it can bear being repeated." [2]

AUTHORITY

The move director must be vested with ultimate authority in all things regarding or influencing the move. Careful selection must be made not to appoint someone who will abuse that authority; but, if the move is to work, the director must have final word. No matter that the chairman of the board has ordered the move to take place on October 15, if the move director has determined that the date is not propitious for the move, his authority must be heeded. It is imperative that, right from the first, all parties agree that the decisions of the move director shall be binding. This does not mean that others may not question his decisions--for that is only wise--but if he refuses to budge, his authority is final.

It must also be made clear from the start that everyone in the library is to cooperate with the move director by doing whatever job he or she is called upon to do to facilitate the move. A move almost invariably means an increased workload for everyone; that fact should be made clear from the outset so that no one will feel he is being unfairly overburdened by this new authority figure.

More often than not, the move director is chosen by default-- because no one else is willing, or because it is a small operation and one person is more dispensable from his regular duties than the others, or because it is a one-person library and there simply is no one else.

In such situations, the move director must prepare himself to personally attend to all aspects of the move, rather than to delegate, and must seek the cooperation of others in the organization whose function lies outside the library. A school librarian, for example, may have to seek help from other faculty members.

---

[2] Kephart, John E. "Moving a Library" *Occasional Papers* (University of Illinois Library School) no. 21, May, 1951.

Above all, the move director in even the most hopeless situation must be able to maintain his optimism. He may have no helpers or too many "chiefs"; it may be his first time to move a library, or it may be the first time this particular library has been moved. But thousands of others have moved a library before now and, at least as far as the research of this author and some-time move director goes, everyone has survived to tell the tale!

ESTABLISHING A MOVE COMMITTEE

The decision to establish a move committee and the qualifications for its members will vary according to the needs of the individual library. The primary purpose for such a committee is to act as a supervisory and advisory body to the move director, to provide several points of view, and to back up the authority of the move director in cases in which that authority is called into question.

Unfortunate as the occurrence may be, experience has shown that the authority of the move director is often called into question and his decisions overridden by those who understand little about the move but who hold a position of higher authority. The move committee gives the director the needed support--clout--when his decisions are questioned and, in case of disagreement, provides a hopefully favorable forum in which he can expound the rationale for his decision(s).

If the library has a small staff, the move committee may be composed of non-librarians and its function may be strictly advisory. On the other hand, in the case of a large library, the move committee may be composed partly or entirely of library staff members, and its purpose may be functional rather than (or as well as) advisory--that is, to serve toward preparation for the move in a practical capacity. Specific tasks may be assigned to the committee or to subcommittees of its members.

In a large library it is more practical to have a number of committees whose responsibility is to carry out specific aspects of the move and their planning, while the officially designated "move committee" has some decision-making authority. There should be some representation from each of these functional committees on the move committee to make sure that all units are aware of what the others are doing. The move committee can serve as a sounding board for the move director. He can use the committee to bounce ideas off of or to provide suggestions when he does not have a ready answer. As in the old adage that "two heads are better than one," so is a committee serving in an advisory capacity more likely to remember all the necessary aspects of planning a move than is one person trying to go it alone.

CHAPTER 2

Preliminary Considerations

HOUSECLEANING

Before beginning to plan for the move, there are a number of preliminary details that should be looked after. Proper attention to these items will help ensure that the move goes smoothly.

First of all, do a good "housecleaning." Get rid of everything possible. The fewer things there are to move, the faster and less expensive the move will be. We will discuss weeding the collection in greater detail in the following chapter, but let us emphasize that weeding prior to the move will greatly facilitate the move.

One of the things to look for in weeding is the number of copies of a given title. Make a determination as to how many copies of a given title are necessary to the collection and proceed to get rid of all extra copies.

Not only should one pay careful attention to the weeding process for books, but also for unnecessary furniture, supplies, and miscellanea. If any items of furniture from the old library will not be used in the new library, get rid of them. It is easier to move them out of the way before moving day than to move them to the new facility during a time which will be extremely busy and then later to have to move them again. Moving the furniture out of the way now will provide extra room to work for those involved in the move.

Also, take inventory of supplies and equipment. If a number of supplies are not used because the library no longer does its own mending, get rid of them. If a worktable is not necessary because the new facility has a built-in counter, get rid of the table. It will greatly simplify the task of moving to get rid of as much as possible now.

Pass the advice along to staff members; have each staff member be responsible for cleaning his or her own work area and desk. Let the housecleaning include personal as well as library-owned items. It might even be a good idea to appoint a day or half a day as "housecleaning day." Having everyone work on the same task simultaneously might make it seem less dull. All undesirable items can be brought to a central location. There, before they are discarded, everyone can look over the pile of "junk" to see if he needs any of the items which someone else has discarded--sort of like a rummage sale in which everything is free; everyone loves a rummage sale, and there are always treasures to be found.

MOVE PLANNING ROOM

It is highly recommended, if at all possible, to assign a given room in the library as the "move planning room." Everything should be removed from this room except materials which will be used in planning and executing-- especially in planning--the move. Ideally, the room can be reserved exclusively for this purpose.

It is recommended that the room be in a quiet location, for it will serve as the "think tank" to the move director and his helpers. It should have a door which is lockable from both the inside and the outside and some measure of soundproofing; how much soundproofing is necessary will, of course, depend upon the location. While the library surely does not want to spend money fixing up an old room before moving to a new one, often little, inexpensive things can be done to add to the feeling of quietness--a piece of old carpet on the floor or nailed on the inside of the door, curtains at the windows, etc.

Don't choose a room which is like a fishbowl, surrounded by windows. Those working here will need to spend a lot of time in concentrated thought and will need to shut themselves completely away from the outside world. The feeling that we are being observed can break the concentration of the best of us. Particularly during the early phases when those in the room are spending a lot of time thinking through the move and not being visibly productive, other workers can become resentful of someone who "does nothing but sit there" while they are swamped with their routine tasks. For fairness to those on both sides, the interior of the room needs to be shut away from outside eyes.

The room should contain a desk for the move director in which he can place only those items he needs for his planning. Also recommended is a counter-height work table around which a group can stand while concentrating on floorplans, maps, and diagrams. A draftsman's drawing board would be ideal.

The room must be equipped with a telephone from which the move director can conduct his business. He will probably spend much of his time on the phone with movers, suppliers, move committee members, and others. It is imperative that it be possible to disconnect the phone or shut off the ringer when the director is in a meeting or needs a period of uninterrupted concentration.

The "move planning room" must be equipped with any necessary supplies to facilitate the planning of the move. These include floorplans of both the old and new libraries in a sufficient number so that separate copies can be marked for different purposes by the move director. There should also be nearby access to a photocopier for making additional copies of materials. An overhead projector with plenty of transparencies will facilitate presentations and planning sessions.

The room should be equipped with calendars--the large planning calendars with squares for writing in tasks and deadlines. If there are several task forces, each group should have its own calendar, with a master copy located in this room for the move director.

There should be bulletin boards in sufficient number that items can be displayed thereon in an orderly fashion. As with the calendars, if there are a number of task forces, each should have its own bulletin board where items to and from the move director can be placed. As well as bulletin boards, there should be chalkboard (marker board) space for plans to be diagrammed and presented to a group during planning sessions.

As it will be the primary location for conducting meetings--at least small group and committee meetings--regarding the move, the room will also need to have a conference table and a sufficient number of chairs to accommodate those who will be meeting there.

Naturally, the room must be lockable so someone doesn't "borrow" the floorplan of the new library and forget to return it. Access to the room should be restricted only to those who require it.

RESPONSIBILITY, INSURANCE, AND SAFETY

The move director will need to look at the safety concerns surrounding the move. If a professional mover is to be hired, he will, in most cases, carry his own liability insurance. But the move director must investigate--or make sure that someone in the hierarchy does--the library's coverage and responsibility during the move.

If volunteer or hired help is to be used, the responsibility in case of accident may lie fully on the shoulders of the library. Someone in the library's employ needs to be aware of the extent of that responsibility and the amount of insurance coverage.

One of the best ways of reducing the library's liability is to take affirmative steps toward safety and prevention. The move director, should walk through every step of the move and try to see it from the point of view of the safety inspector. Even better is for two people to do a walk-through together while discussing safety concerns.

Is the building finished, or will it be by moving day? If not, what construction materials (scaffolding, etc.) will constitute safety hazards? Where does the liability of the construction company stop and that of the library begin?

What about stairways? Are stairways complete and handrails installed? If carpeting is to be installed later, is the currently exposed surface slippery, or might it be in case of rain or snow on moving day?

How much dust will be produced on moving day? If the library is an old one which has not had a thorough cleaning for a long time--in referring to dust accumulation, six months is a long time--there will be a considerable amount. Workers with dust-sensitive allergies should be warned and given permission to stay at home on moving day. In hiring workers or volunteers, the library needs to make sure that those with a sensitivity to dust are forewarned. Bear in mind that many non-librarians think that libraries are such nice, clean places to work in, but anyone who has dealt with gift materials can belie this popular fallacy.

If booktrucks or dollies are going to be used for the move, the move director should look at potential trouble spots where one might turn over. The weight of a fully loaded booktruck falling uncontrolled can easily cause serious injury.

A major consideration is unstable stacks. Presumably, the stacks in the new library will be firmly based; if not, it is the move director's responsibility to see that they are firm before ever consenting that the move take place. Again, it must be emphasized that he must be vested with sufficient authority to make this kind of decision and not budge until the situation has been remedied. All stacks should be firmly anchored by transversal beams attached at the top and running perpendicular to the rows. These channels are commercially available from the same suppliers as the bookstacks.

The stacks in the old library, however, may be quite unstable. It is not to be expected that the library spend a great deal of money installing transversal channels on stacks that are soon to be disassembled or even discarded. But there are some positive steps the library can take to ensure safety.

First of all, if the stacks are tipsy, those working there must be warned of the situation before the moving process and frequently during the process. The exercise of adequate care can prevent a costly accident. Because it is easy to place concentration on the task at hand--moving--at the exclusion of all else, workers need to be reminded frequently during the move to be safety conscious. It is wise to have a supervisor, or several, simply to observe that movers are following good safety procedures.

A second, and extremely important, step which can be taken to protect the well-being of the movers is the exercise of care in the order in which stacks are unloaded. It goes without saying--or should--that stacks are to be unloaded from top to bottom so that the center of gravity remains low.[1] The other important consideration

---

[1] Unfortunately, the reverse--to load the bottom of the stack before loading the top--is not usually possible in the new location. Because books tend to be shelved in call number order, most frequently, the top shelves are filled first. However, proper

in loading and unloading stacks is that both sides of the stack should be loaded or unloaded simultaneously, thus keeping an approximately equal amount of weight on each side. The reader may, at this point, wonder how it is possible to do this and still keep the books in proper order. If the move has been properly planned, as will be discussed in later chapters, this will not present any problem as far as keeping the materials in sequence is concerned.

SECURITY OF THE COLLECTION

The security of the collection must be of prime concern, particularly if rare or valuable books are to be moved. Because access to both the new and the old buildings is relatively uncontrolled on moving day(s), it is often quite easy for anyone to gain entrance. It is rather ironic that we spend thousands of dollars to install a security system to protect our materials and then on move day throw the doors wide open to any and all.

One of the best methods of prevention of theft is to have a sufficient number of supervisors whose job is simply to serve as monitors--not strictly as anti-theft monitors, of course, but whose function is solely to observe all that goes on during move day and to help eliminate any potential problems, theft or otherwise.

Each supervisor should have some type of badge or armband which distinctly identifies him and his rank. Each mover should also have some identifying badge. If a supervisor sees someone who is not a fellow supervisor entering the new library without carrying a load of books, or, worse yet, leaving the new library *carrying* a load of books, he should be stopped and his behavior questioned. If movers are walking between the two buildings carrying loads of books and someone is observed walking off the assigned walkway, his behavior should be questioned.

---

anchoring of the stack via the transversal channels and ordinary caution and common sense can help minimize the risk.

If, as is often the case, the supervisors themselves are students or young people, provision should be made for them to locate quickly and discreetly someone with the proper authority. On the other hand, while theft of materials is quite possible on moving day, cited incidents of its occurring are rare. However, it is difficult to say whether that fact is attributable to non-occurrence or to the difficulty of tracing the disappearance of materials to moving day.

Of course, it must also be remembered that things get topsy turvy on move day, and unless a thief has planned his actions well, it just might not be possible to walk into the building and locate a favorite book on the shelf where it has always stood. Therefore, he must either look up a call number in the card catalog--which may not be available--or have memorized or prerecorded the call number. Someone browsing through the stacks apparently looking for a certain call number on move day would constitute unusual behavior and certainly be cause for suspicion. Possibly it is for this reason that book thefts on moving day, while not impossible, are probably rare. Naturally, the risk factor will vary greatly with the environment and type of library.

FLOW OF THE MOVE

It is during the period prior to the move that the move director should, in his mind, walk through each step of the move. He must locate potential bottlenecks and do whatever is possible to eliminate them.

It must be borne in mind that the move will proceed no faster than the slowest bottleneck. The move director must watch particularly for traffic flow. Will movers be crossing paths with each other? Crossed paths should be avoided if at all possible, even if one group must follow a longer route to avoid it. Remember that the longer route should be reserved for those making the return trip, not those who are carrying materials.

If boxes are moving down a stairway from an upper level, how will the empty boxes be returned to that level? Will the traffic flow have to stop for a few minutes every hour to allow the empties to travel up the stairs? Will the process be disruptive? If so, an alternative should be sought.

Remember that it is difficult to carry a burden up or down stairs-- more so when the number of books per person is increased by using boxes or troughs. Stairways also add an element of danger and should be avoided whenever possible. If an alternative to the stairway can be found, the stairway can be reserved for using the bucket brigade method to return empty boxes to the upper levels without interfering with the traffic flow.

Fortunate is the library with elevators in both its new and old buildings. A more common scenario is an elevator in the new building but none in the old. In any case, unless its use is carefully scheduled, an elevator can present a major bottleneck in the smooth flow of materials.

Before the move begins, the move director needs to time the flow of materials and schedule them to arrive at the elevator when it has returned to the proper floor and is ready to receive a load. This planning will be especially difficult if an elevator is used to load or unload several floors simultaneously. Schedules must be tightly adhered to.

Another consideration in using elevators is their load limit. Books, en masse, tend to be heavier than people, and the weight limit of an elevator can be quickly exceeded. Prior to moving day, the move director must discover what that weight limit is and must measure the weight of a fully loaded dolly or booktruck. He must then make known the limits of the elevator in practical terms, such as: "MAXIMUM LOAD: Three dollies and two people." These limits should be posted conspicuously near the elevator door on each floor.

Many libraries, however, have no elevator. What, then, are the alternatives? Building a ramp from an upper story window may be a great time saver. The cost of the ramp is often offset by the savings in time, and, thus, in wages paid to hired help. Part of the cost can also be offset by the savings in wear-and-tear on materials that may be dropped if the stairs are used. Or again, because using a ramp is less tiring, each worker's output will tend to be greater, thus producing more for the money. And a ramp may result in a considerable savings by avoiding a lawsuit as the result of an accident that could have happened if the stairs had been used.

A professional mover can be hired to build the ramp, whether or not he is hired to complete the rest of the move. Or, a ramp can be built by a private contractor. Libraries which are part of a larger institution have the advantage that often there is a maintenance crew which can be used to build the ramp. Or, the task may be given to the *Friends of the Library*.

In the case of a lower level where books must be brought up to ground level, or in transporting the materials to an upper level in the new building, a conveyer system may be the best choice. Conveyor systems can be rented from Rent-all outlets. Libraries in rural areas may be fortunate enough to be able to borrow a conveyor from a local farmer or co-op.

A conveyor system has an advantage over a ramp in that conveyor systems, often built on wheels, are usually readily portable. Depending on how the move is planned, a single conveyor system may be moved back and forth between locations to remove books from an upper level of the old library and then to transport them to an upper level of the new building. Another advantage of a conveyor system is that the belt can be reversed to return the empty cartons to the upper levels of the old building when not bringing the full ones down.

Construction companies will occasionally build an elevator outside the wall of the building to facilitate the transport of construction materials. It is possible that an arrangement can be made with the contractor for this elevator to remain in place until after the move.

Other libraries which have many materials to remove from an upper floor without a good traffic pattern may want to consider having a construction-type elevator built for the duration of the move. These elevators can often be built outside an upper level window, greatly facilitating the flow of materials. Local construction companies can be hired to construct the elevator. Because the construction company actually owns the elevator and is, in essence, renting it to the library, the cost may not be as prohibitive at is would seem. Particularly during the winter months when the construction industry is not doing much outside work, they may be glad to find some use for their equipment and their workers. Again, the move director must investigate the library's liability and insurance coverage for the use of such an elevator.

INTER-BUILDING COMMUNICATION

A primary concern is inter-building communication. On move day, there needs to be a head supervisor in the old location and one in the new location whose function is to regulate the flow of materials. These supervisors must be able to communicate with one another. If there is a delay in shelving reference materials in the new building, for instance, the supervisor there needs to tell the supervisor in the old library to stop sending reference materials and to concentrate on bound periodicals instead.

Sending a runner back and forth may be too time consuming--or altogether impossible if the buildings are located some distance apart. Messengers are also liable to garble the message--as in the children's game of "telephone" --unless the sender resorts to written communication. Written communication may just not be possible under the circumstances of moving day.

Therefore, it is imperative that telephone, or telephone type, communication be available between the two locations on moving day. The move director should delay the move until such communication is available and has been tested.

As the move supervisors are highly mobile, it is unlikely that they will be, at a given moment, near a specific phone extension. The best solution may be a cordless phone. Now available at prices that are quite reasonable, a cordless phone should be easy to acquire. In view of the number of potential snags they may eliminate, a library may consider that the price of a pair of cordless phones is a small portion of the total move budget. The phones may later be used in the new library where they may prove particularly useful to the reference staff in answering telephone queries. Or, in the case of a school or small special library where there is no phone in either the new or the old location, a cordless may provide a temporary phone for moving day.

As with all other systems, the cordless phone should be installed and tested well in advance of moving day. The first factor to consider is the compatibility of the cordless phone with the current phone system. A pulse (rotary) dial cordless phone may not function with a true tone phone system while a true tone cordless phone may not function with a pulse system. Many of the newer models of cordless phones are switchable, being completely compatible with either type of phone system.

Large libraries or those which are part of a larger institution may have a computerized phone system. Some cordless phones may not be compatible with such a system or may not allow full use of its features.[2] The move director should check with the person in charge of communications at the institution to see if a cordless phone is compatible with the system.

Because cordless phones operate on radio frequencies, they are subject to influence by and interference from a number of outside factors. One of these is the type of building construction.

Because libraries are built to withstand a great deal of weight, large amounts of steel and concrete are used in their construction. The steel, especially, may interfere with communication by cordless telephone.

Another factor that may interfere with communications via cordless phone is the operation of computer terminals (e.g. OCLC terminals). Test the phone for interference from this source by using it with the terminals both on and off. If, as will probably be true in most cases, the terminals will be inoperative and turned off on moving day(s), any interference can be disregarded.

Perhaps the most common source of interference for cordless phones is fluorescent lighting. Fluorescent lights often produce a great deal of hum or static on the frequencies at which a cordless phone operates. In most cases, all lights in both the old and new buildings will be operative on moving day, so any interference produced thereby must be taken seriously. Often the interference is

---

[2] One such feature is the "flash" feature, which allows the transfer of calls from one extension to another.

great enough to render communication all but impossible. Because of the amount of noise going on around the speaker and listener on moving day, they may be totally unable to carry on a conversation if the signal is anything but loud and clear. It is imperative that the lighting in the new building be installed and operative when the phones are tested.

Because, by law, most elevators contain a telephone for emergency purposes, an elevator may be a good communications center for a move supervisor. If the elevator is not in frequent use for the move, it can be moved from floor to floor as the supervisor moves.

The elevator may also provide a convenient location for the connection of the base unit of a cordless phone. As the elevator can be moved from floor to floor, the base unit can be kept close to the the handset, thus improving the range and quality of communication.

The installation of a cordless phone will require a modular plug which is now the standard for all telephone installations.[3] Bear in mind that the installation of a cordless phone also requires a standard electrical outlet--usually three-pronged--for the base unit. If the cordless phone is to be installed in an elevator, it is likely that there will be no electrical outlet there. However, because electricity is present for operation of the lights and fan, the installation of an outlet can be a relatively simple process.

Once the cordless phones are properly installed, the move director should find a colleague to help him test the communications network. While carrying on a telephone conversation with each other, one person in each of the library buildings should go to every area in that building where a supervisor might possibly have need of going on move day, including the basement, the roof, and

---

[3] While a modular plug will probably be the standard in the new building, it may not yet be the standard in the old building, thus requiring additional modification for the installation of a cordless phone. Such modifications are usually simple, quick, and inexpensive (under ten dollars for a do-it-yourself operation).

stairways. Communication should be clear and effortless. Both phones should be checked for their ability to receive and place calls from any location.

An alternative to the telephone is the walkie-talkie. Larger libraries and those which are part of a larger institution may already have walkie-talkies available for their use. Advantages of walkie-talkies are that they require no installation and that several people may join the conversation simultaneously. Again, the walkie-talkies should be tested in plenty of time before the move and from every possible location.

Another option is the wireless headset. Libraries which form part of a larger institution may find headsets available at no charge elsewhere in their institution. Theater groups often use headsets of this type for the director to communicate with the stage manager, the prop people and the lighting crew. Academic libraries should check for the availability of headsets with their theater department, and other libraries might want to check with a local theater group.

The battery operated power unit is usually clipped to the belt and connected to the headset via a cable. Advantages of the headset over the phone are its hands-free operation and the fact that many headsets may listen in on the same frequency. A decided disadvantage is the relatively limited range. Some headsets may not function from building to building, and certainly not if the two libraries are a considerable distance apart.

The move director should begin early to search for the best possible means of communication and should test each one until finding one that works correctly and effortlessly.

CHAPTER 3

Weeding

Because moving a library is a task of such magnitude, every effort possible should be made to reduce the work load. Of all methods for reducing the load, the most obvious is to reduce the number of items to be moved.

A careful inventory must be made of what the needs will be in the new library. Will new furniture be ordered to match the new decor? If so, will the old be discarded? Then, why move it?

Is the library installing an automated catalog that will replace the card catalog? Then, why move it?

Will word processors replace the old typewriters? Then, leave them behind.

Are new stereo systems being installed in the listening rooms in the new library which will replace the portable cassette players now in use? Then, leave them behind.

The same rule holds true for books. It is a wise choice to leave behind or to discard before the move those books which are soon to be weeded from the collection.

Because space in the old library may well have been at a premium for years, many libraries have maintained a vigorous weeding program. Unfortunately, this is not universally the case. If there are materials in the collection that need to be weeded, weed them now, before the move.

Weeding must be carried on in such a way that it does not interfere with the planning for the move. Because the move is very energy absorbing, weeding should be carried on, if at all possible, by those not already overworked with preparations for the move. In a smaller library where a limited number of staff perform all tasks, weeding should be carried on far enough in advance of the move that it can be completed before the move begins to absorb everyone's energy.

School, academic and some special libraries have an advantage over public libraries in the weeding process in that they may be able to involve faculty members or employees from other departments who are not directly related to the move, thus lightening the load for the library staff. Each faculty member or employee is responsible for reviewing the holdings in his or her area of expertise and making recommendations to the library staff for weeding.

A weeding technique which has worked particularly well in academic settings is what this author calls the "Lois Luesing Technique."[1]   With administrative support, each academic department is made responsible for weeding a certain section of the library, according to its area of expertise, at some time during the academic year prior to the move. The weeding is done by the department as a group, with all members required to be in the library at the same time. In order to avoid making the job unmanageable by having more than one division in the library at the same time, at the beginning of the year, each department chooses two consecutive days during an academic break at which time the library is closed, or at least, when usage is comparatively low.

The library staff makes preparations in advance by providing the necessary materials. The department head is given a list of the stack areas (by call number) for which his department is responsible. The department head then assigns specific stack areas to specific faculty members, preferably according to their areas of teaching responsibility. The faculty members spend the day in the stack area(s) assigned to them. Breaks are taken as a group, with refreshments provided by the library staff.

Each faculty member is given a sheet of self-adhesive paper dots. The dots should be red or some other highly visible color. Each time the faculty member finds a book he feels should be weeded, he sticks a dot on the spine of the book just above the call number.

---

[1] Lois Luesing is library director at Asbury College in Wilmore, Kentucky.

After the department has finished its area, and before the library has been reopened to borrowers, affording them the opportunity to maliciously move the dots around, library staff members read the stacks with the shelflist in hand. The shelflist card for each dotted book is pulled from the drawer and set aside.

At their convenience, the professional librarians responsible for collection development can go through the stack of shelflist cards and make the final decision on whether or not a certain title should be weeded.

Many faculty members react to this technique by saying, "I really objected to having to give up some of my vacation days, but I'm glad I did. I learned about a lot of things which support my courses that I didn't know we had in the library. Besides, it was a lot of fun for all of us to get together."

Although faculty members often regard their breaks as vacation days, they are usually considered by the administration as preparation time for teaching assignments, and that time can thus legitimately be designated by an administrator as time to be spent in the library. For this technique to be successful, it is imperative that the library staff have a good working relationship with the administration so that they will support it.

The weeded materials can often be sold via a booksale to students or the public with the proceeds used to help buy replacement materials or to help finance the cost of the move.

Even if it is not possible to weed on such an intensive scale, weeding of some sort should be carried out. Every book that is moved from the old to the new library will add to the amount of energy, time, and expense of the move--which, at best, is already a costly project.

CHAPTER 4

Planning for expansion

DETERMINING THE SIZE OF THE COLLECTION.

Before any planning can be made for the move of the collection, an accurate determination must be made of its size. Two totally different measurements of the collection must be taken: The volume count and the collection size in linear feet. For such things as contracting with a professional mover, a reasonably exact volume count may be necessary. For planning the actual move, however, the total number of linear feet of books to be moved is far more useful than a volume count.

This linear figure is very important in determining how much shelving will have to be available to house the collection at the new location. Therefore, measurements will probably need to be determined long in advance of the move--before ordering shelving for the new building.

Obtaining a volume count.

Several methods can be used for arriving at an accurate figure of the number of volumes to be moved:

A. Actual count.

Most libraries are fairly accurate in keeping statistics of their collections. If record keeping has been carefully done, it is simply a matter of checking the files to determine how many items are on hand. Often, this is broken down by categories, such as books, bound periodicals, filmstrips, phonograph records, reels of microfilm, etc. Some libraries may be able to determine the number of volumes in a given special collection or within a subdivision such as the Dewey 920s, etc. The more accurate the count and the greater the number of subdivisions it is broken into, the easier the planning for the move.

In the event that an exact count is not available, it is often possible to make a fair estimate of collection size based on the highest accession number in use. From this number, subtract the number of volumes that have been weeded or lost, provided such information is available or can be estimated, and the result should be quite close to an actual count.

A more difficult, yet far more accurate method, is to physically count the volumes. Though tedious, such a task is not infeasible, even in a large collection, if there is sufficient lead time and staff so that the job may be divided into manageable portions. Because of its greater degree of reliability, this method should be used wherever possible.

If the library is open for use during the time of the counting, many volumes may be missed because they are in circulation, pulled for mending, etc. There are two ways to avoid this problem:

1) Count the number of volumes physically present on the shelves in a given area. Instruct all personal that inventory is being conducted in that area and that they are not to reshelve any materials for the time being. Having obtained the shelf count, add the number of volumes on the truck ready to be shelved in that area. Determine the number of volumes currently in circulation by counting the borrowers' cards and add this number to the count. Some volumes are sure to be left uncounted as they may be pulled for processing or repair, in someone's office, or in use elsewhere within the library. Therefore, bear in mind that by using the shelf count method, any inaccuracy will probably result in an underestimation of the actual number of volumes owned by the library.

2) Use the shelflist cards to count the volumes. Be sure to count each volume of a set as an individual volume when sets are listed on the same card. The same applies when multiple copies of the same work are listed on a single card. Care must also be taken not to count multiple cards when a single work runs onto more than one card. Counting the shelflist, however, does not allow for books

which are lost or missing, whether or not that loss has yet been noted on the card. Though *lost* books do not often return, they sometimes do; *missing* books do so with greater frequency. Books whose loss has not yet been discovered will be mistakenly added to the count. Thus, by using the shelflist method, any inaccuracy will probably result in an overestimation of the actual number of volumes owned by the library. Overestimation, at least, is a less serious error than underestimation.

B. Estimate.

Many libraries, particularly larger ones, and especially those which have inadequate staff, will sometimes have to resort to an estimate if accurate records are not readily available. There are several methods for making an estimate.

The move director who is not versed in sampling and statistical methods would be well advised to do some background reading in that area. Random sampling techniques are not random at all but are based on sampling every Nth specimen, a specific number apart. The most accurate sampling techniques advise the use of a random number table, which can be purchased commercially.

Libraries that have access to microcomputers can use them to generate random numbers; many micros have a built in function for producing random numbers. Consult the owner's manual for each particular brand of hardware.

The larger a sample is, the more time-consuming it will be to conduct the research, but the more accurate the sample will be in representing the whole. Libraries are well advised to use the largest sample that their time and budget will allow.

1) The first method involves taking a random sample of shelves in the collection which is to be moved. On each shelf in the sample, count the actual number of books. Add together the number of volumes on all shelves in the sample and divide the total by the number of shelves in the sample to get an estimate of volumes per shelf. Then, multiply the total number of shelves in the collection to be moved by this estimated number of volumes per shelf.

2) Another method, perhaps less accurate but faster, is to estimate the number of volumes which fit on a full library shelf and then multiply by the percentage of occupancy, which can be "guesstimated" by a fairly quick visual tour of the stacks. That is, if a small sample shows that approximately 30 books fit on a full shelf and the shelves are 90% full, the average number of books per shelf for the collection is 27. Then, multiply 27 by the total number of shelves to be moved to get an approximate volume count.

3) It is also possible, though less accurate, to estimate the size of the collection from the shelflist. Take a random sample of the shelflist by measuring one inch of cards at various places in the shelflist. Be sure to include different subject areas in the sample. Count the number of volumes represented in one inch of cards.[1] Add together the total number of books represented in each inch and divide by the total number of inches sampled to get an approximate number of volumes per inch. Be sure to count separately multiple copies of the same work listed on one card and multi-volume works cataloged as a set. Each individual volume must be counted. It might even be desirable to count completely, rather than sample, some specific areas such as Reference to eliminate inaccuracies due to such complications. Finally, the entire shelflist should be measured in inches. Multiply the length of the shelflist (in inches) by the number of volumes per inch, as previously determined in the sample, to obtain a reasonably accurate estimate of the total number of volumes in the collection.

---

[1] A standard estimate is 100 cards per inch, but this figure can vary so considerably depending on such factors as thickness of the card stock, number of volumes per card, etc., that each library should determine its own figure.

DETERMINING THE LENGTH OF THE COLLECTION

The best method for determining the length of the collection to be moved in linear feet is to take a physical measurement. This method should be used if at all possible. When actual measurement is not possible, a fairly accurate estimate can be obtained using one of several methods:

1) It is usually a fairly quick task to determine the number of shelves holding the collection by counting the rows of stacks in the library and the number of stacks per row. Then count the number of shelves per stack (usually seven or eight per side) and the length of a shelf in inches. Estimate the percentage of occupancy, that is to say, what percent of the shelf is holding books. Percentage of occupancy x length of shelf x shelves per stack x stacks per row x number of rows = length of collection.

2) An estimate of the length of the collection can be obtained via a technique similar to the shelflist method mentioned previously. Sample several random one-inch blocks of shelflist cards, noting the bibliographic data of the first and last volume in each block. Then, physically go to the stacks with a tape measure to determine the number of linear feet of books between the first and last book in the block. Naturally, this is best done when the library is closed and all or most of the books are on the shelf. If a number of books are in circulation, allow for the space they would normally occupy as nearly as can be determined. Do not push books together when there is an empty space on the shelf. When an accurate sample has been obtained, multiply the number of linear feet of books represented by one inch of shelflist cards by the total number of inches of the shelflist.

For example, Paul Schneider, a clerk at Mytown Library measured one inch of its shelflist. Noting the bibliographic data of the first and last books represented in the block of cards, he went to the stack and found those two books. With a tape measure, he measured all the occupied shelf space between and including the first and the last book. He repeated this process a number of times in random locations. When enough data had been obtained, he added up the total number of linear feet of books and divided by the number of inches measured in the shelflist for the sample. He discovered that the average measurement was 13.75 feet of books per inch of shelflist. He then measured the total shelflist, 526 inches, and multiplied the result by 13.75 feet. Thus, the collection of Mytown Library contains 7,232.5 linear feet of books.

There are two methods of planning the quantity of shelving for the new location. The two methods are ideologically opposed. Ideally, it will be possible to order all the shelving necessary to house the collection and allow room for expansion. In this case, it is necessary to determine the length of the collection and how many linear feet of books will optimally be placed on each stack at the end of the move.

A general rule of thumb is to consider seven shelves per stack face. The top and bottom shelves remain empty to allow room for expansion and because they are the most inaccessible to the average user. Of the five remaining occupied shelves, one third of each shelf should also remain empty for expansion. Therefore, seven shelves minus top and bottom shelves equals five shelves. One shelf equals approximately three feet. Three feet minus 1/3 equals two feet. Two feet times five shelves equals ten feet of books per stack face.

Having determined the total number of linear feet of books in the collection, divide by ten. The result is the number of stack faces needed in the new library. The exact location of shelving in each individual situation will determine the number of single sided stacks and the number of double sided stacks which should be ordered.

If a library wishes to house more or fewer books per stack, the figures will change, but the amount of shelving can be calculated exactly as above:

Total linear feet in collection
-------------------------------   = number of stacks needed.
linear feet of books per stack face (after move)

A library which is limited in the amount of shelf space available in the new location, can use a similar method for determining the number of books to be housed on each shelf:
First determine the linear footage of the new shelving available. Divide the linear footage of the current collection by the linear footage of the total new shelving. The result will be the percentage of occupancy we must have on each shelf after the move.
For example, let's say our (very small) current collection has three stacks of seven three-foot shelves each of which is 100% occupied--63 linear feet of books--and the new location has five stacks of seven three-foot shelves--105 linear feet of shelving available.

$$\frac{63 \text{ (current length)}}{105 \text{ (available length)}} = .6 \ (60\%)$$

Each shelf in the new library must be 60% occupied, that is, it must contain 1.8 feet of books. (Check: 1.8 feet of books x 35 shelves = 63 linear feet of books--the current collection.)
In the above example, if we wanted to leave the top and bottom shelves vacant for expansion, we would figure five stacks x five shelves x three feet = 75 linear feet of shelving available.

$$\frac{63 \text{ feet of books}}{75 \text{ feet of new shelving}} = .84 \ (84\%)$$

Three feet x 84% = 2.52 feet of books per shelf. (Check: 2.52 feet of books per shelf x 25 available shelves = 63 feet of books--the current collection.)
Certain areas (e.g. quarto volumes, bound periodicals) must be given special consideration. Because of the extra height of the volumes, fewer shelves must often be placed on each stack face. Other than that, the method for determining the necessary amount of shelving is identical to the method used for any other section.

LENGTH OF TIME NEEDED FOR MOVE.

Prior studies of the amount of time required by libraries to move a given number of volumes prove only that moving rates are extremely inconsistent. There are simply too many variables to plan the timing of a future move based on someone else's experience. Variables such as distance, terrain, method of moving, number of workers, number and size of volumes, stamina of workers, the weather, and even the type of library building are so different from one situation to another that no generalities can be drawn.

The best method for determining the amount of time needed for the move of a given library is a time-and-motion study. In order for a time-and-motion study to be accurate, however, the sample must be sufficiently large and must therefore include several trial runs. Smaller libraries would be wise to forgo the time-and-motion study as not being cost effective; by expending the same amount of time and energy necessary to achieve an accurate sample, they can often move a large portion of their collection.

Larger libraries will probably want to conduct the study. Each task in the process of getting a book from shelf A in the old location to shelf B in the new location must be isolated and timed. These tasks will vary from library to library, but most generally are: Removing the book from shelf A and packing it (if containers are used), transporting the container to the point of loading onto a vehicle, loading the container onto the vehicle, moving the loaded vehicle (if vehicles are used), unloading the container from the vehicle, transporting the container to stack B, unpacking and shelving the book, returning the empty container to the loading dock, loading the container onto the vehicle, transporting the container, unloading the container from the vehicle, and returning the container to stack A.

The length of time required for each of these tasks will vary greatly even within the same library. It will take longer to move 100 quarto volumes, for example, than to move the same number of fiction books simply because fewer of the large quarto volumes fit into each container and more containers will have to be moved. It might take longer to move the literature books than the science books because the literature books are on the third floor while the science collection is housed on ground level. It might take longer to transport the reference collection than it does the periodical indexes because the reference books go to the back of the new building while the indexes go near the front entrance. In addition to such factors, we must allow for differences in worker strength and stamina.

Based on the figures obtained in the time-and-motion study, a plan must be formulated for obtaining the optimum number of workers and the proper types and number of pieces of equipment.

The larger library may also wish to use the study for determining the best of alternate courses of action. Is it best to have several pickup trucks in constant circulation, or is it faster to have one or two large trucks wait for a full load? Is it better to return the empty cartons by reversing the conveyor belt or to keep the conveyor carrying full cartons while the empties are toted back up the stairs? Would a smaller group of workers be easier to control than a large group who tend to get in each other's way?

With so many factors to consider, a large library will probably find the time-and-motion study a useful tool while it would be too time consuming for a smaller library.

Regardless of size, in preparing for a move, any library must determine some reasonably accurate figures for the number of volumes to be moved, the number of linear feet in the collection, and the length of time necessary for the move.

CHAPTER 5

Handling periodicals.

Without a doubt, the most difficult part of the collection to move is the bound periodicals. Periodicals are different from books because they grow differently. To allow room for expansion in the appropriate places, their move must be plotted even more carefully than that of the books.

CURRENT PERIODICALS

The most common reason for moving a library is overcrowding of the old facility. However, overcrowding poses a far more serious problem in the areas of books and bound periodicals than it does in current periodicals. Increases in the current periodicals section are usually planned more to provide room for the patron than for the periodicals themselves.

The reason is simple: Current periodicals collections do not tend to grow. The only way a library increases its need to add more shelf space for current periodicals is by adding more subscriptions; generally, the number of subscriptions remains somewhat static (particularly in times of limited budgets), and so does the need for shelf space in this area. The need for increased space in the new facility in the area of current periodicals tends to be rather small compared to the need for space in other areas.

Because of these relatively unchanging space needs and because this particular collection tends to be comparatively small, it is one of the easiest parts of the collection to move. Because of their differences in growth and space needs, the treatment for moving current periodicals may be quite different from that afforded to bound periodicals.

The first key to moving current periodicals is to clear the shelves of as many loose issues as possible before the move. Moves in January and July are especially convenient because many complete volumes can be shipped away to the bindery before the move with specific instructions not to return them until after the moving date and then, to the new location. In no other area of the library is it possible to simply rid oneself of a great portion of the collection before approaching the move. Of the issues which are not being sent to the bindery, as many as possible should be boxed (if that is the custom of the library) and moved to the bound shelves.

There are two good ways to move the remaining issues:

ALPHABETICALLY BY TITLE. Place the issues in order in packing cartons. When the first carton is full, start the second carton, etc. Number the cartons sequentially. Start from the end of the alphabet and work backwards. The advantage of this technique is that the titles nearest the beginning of the alphabet will end up near the top of each carton, and those cartons will end up on top of the piles of cartons. The unpacker only needs to remember to unpack the highest numbered carton first and proceed in reverse order. If current periodicals are classified and shelved by call number, the system works just as well by packing those with the highest call number first.

BY LOCATION CODE. While the alphabetical method works well when the amount of shelf space is approximately the same in the old and new libraries, it may not be ideal when shelf space for current periodical titles is increasing.

Draw up a diagram of the shelves in the new location. Assign each shelf a location code, for example, row H, stack 1, shelf 5. For each title assign, on paper, a specific shelf on which it will rest in the new location.

Before the move, pace a self-stick label with a code corresponding to the *new* shelf under each magazine in the *old* location. On moving day, as each box is packed, write its location code on the top, and the box can be delivered directly to that location in the new building. This method permits moving any part of the alphabet first or last, in or out of sequence.

An increasing number of libraries employ word processors or database programs for serials control. If possible, take advantage of such programs to generate a self-adhesive label for each current periodical title. Affix each label to the destination shelf for that title in the new building. After the move, the labels will continue to be useful to shelvers in returning the magazines to their proper place. For this reason, even if the labels must be individually hand-typed, most libraries will find that it is well worth the time and effort invested.

When shelf space is increasing greatly and/or space must be left for a number of new titles being added to the collection, an adaptation of the method detailed below for bound periodicals will serve well.

BOUND PERIODICALS.

When a building is new, it may seem that it is going to last forever and will be the library's permanent home. However distasteful it may be to think of moving again while still planning the first move, realistically speaking, libraries, unlike diamonds, are not forever. Any library that is expanding will eventually outgrow its allotted space. The question must be honestly asked, therefore, in planning for the move: How many years does the library expect to be in the new building before additional space becomes available either through expansion or building anew?

Because bound periodicals can gobble up shelf space at an astounding rate, before planning for expansion space for shelving them, it is important to know how many years of a given title a library will be expected to shelve before the facility is expanded. This need will vary greatly depending on the type of library. A small public library, for example, which weeds all (or most) of its bound periodicals after five years from the date of issue will not need nearly the shelf space of a major research library which keeps complete runs of back volumes of thousands of titles.

The next question the move director must ask is how many years a subscription is likely to be continued. If, for example, several subscriptions serve to please the employees of a nearby major manufacturer which has just announced that it is closing its local plant and transferring its employees elsewhere, those subscriptions will probably soon be dropped. It would then be unnecessary to leave expansion space for ten years' growth of those titles.

Another consideration is the likelihood of a magazine's future availability. In the case of a popular magazine supporting a specific brand of personal computer, if that computer has recently stopped being manufactured, it is likely (but not guaranteed) that the magazine will soon cease publication. If the title is not one that is likely to suspend publication, are the issues likely to grow in height or thickness? Are they likely to increase or decrease in frequency? It seems to be a trend that a number of scholarly journals of limited readership, in the name of cutting costs, are reducing their frequency from monthly to quarterly publications (while their subscription prices increase, of course). All these factors will determine the amount of shelf space needed to accommodate future growth. As the move director often does not have the foreknowledge to predict such things, he or she must do his or her best with the information available and expect that some errors will be made. The goal is to keep their number to an absolute minimum.

In planning for expansion, it is important to note the difference in the growth pattern of books and bound periodicals. The book collection can expand at any given point at any time; it can grow forward, backward, or in the middle, depending on the classification number of the new acquisitions. In most cases, periodicals grow only forward, only at the end of a run, only from left to right, top to bottom. If a library has a complete run of *Saturday Evening Post* from 1942 to date, that collection will grow only as the library adds new volumes from the latest volumes forward. The 1942 volumes, therefore, can be placed at a fixed point from which they will be moved with rare exception. Any growth room should be planned from the current date forward--at the end of the run.

There are two exceptions to the above rule:

1) There are gaps in the collection which will be filled in later, e.g. the years 1953-57 are missing. In the book collection, it is often difficult to predict where growth will occur, but in periodicals, such gaps are readily visible and can be anticipated.

2) There is a gap in the collection preceding the current run, e.g. volumes published before 1942. Again, these gaps are readily visible, and growth of this type can usually be planned for in advance.

Bound periodicals are also unlike books in that oversize volumes are encountered more frequently.

For the above reasons, in planning for the move of bound periodicals, several types of exact measurements are necessary: First of all, determine the height of the tallest volume of a particular title. Then, measure the thickness of each volume.

The height will determine how many shelves to place on a stack side, which is usually fewer than the customary seven used in the bookstacks.

After measuring the thickness of a volume of each title, multiply that thickness by the number of bound volumes per year to determine how much that title will grow in one year. Then decide how many years' growth space to leave for each title.

A form for recording the data on each title will be extremely valuable. Figure 5-1 shows a suggested form for a 3 x 5 card.

There are two methods of plotting how many years' growth to leave for each title. The first, and best, of these methods is based on need. Determine how many years the library will occupy the new facility before expanding or undertaking another move. Then, leave room for that many years' growth for each title.

The other method, far from ideal, but often more realistic, is based on the amount of space available in the new facility. In this method, the number of linear feet of space available is divided by the number of linear feet that the collection grows in a year. The result gives the number of years' growth room that can be left for each title.

```
|Title                        |From (yr):      To:     |
|                             |                        |
|_____|_____|
|Height (in.)       |Thickness (in.)                   |
|                   |                                  |
|_____|_____|
|Closed        |Open    |                              |
|entry         |entry        |Retained for ....   years|
|Length of present run (ft. & in.)                     |
|                                                      |
|_____|
|                                                      |
|1 year's growth (in inches) ---------------           |
|                                                      |
|  x number of yrs to leave for growth -----           |
|                                                      |
| = amount of empty shelves to leave (in.)             |
```

(fig 5-1)

Once the information for each title is obtained and placed on the forms illustrated in figure 5-1, a simple mathematical formula completes the planning. The formula for expansion based on need is:

$$cc + (yg * ye) = ns$$

$$
\begin{aligned}
cc &= \text{current collection (length)} \\
yg &= \text{one year's growth (length)} \\
ye &= \text{number of years expected in current location} \\
ns &= \text{needed shelving (length)}
\end{aligned}
$$

The formula for plotting the amount of expansion room which can be left for each title when there is a definite limit to the amount of available shelving varies slightly:

$$
\begin{aligned}
ts - cc &= as \\
as / yg &= yt
\end{aligned}
$$

ts = total available shelving (length)
cc = current collection (length)
as = available shelving for growth (length)
yg = one year's growth (length)
yt = years of growth room per title (length)

If the library has a computer available, the data for each title can be entered into a database and a simple formula written for calculating either of the two figures. Thus, if any of the information needs to be changed as plans for the move progress, there will not be a need for a lengthy manual recalculation after each change. When the Health Sciences Library at the University of North Carolina at Chapel Hill moved its periodical collection in 1980, those in charge felt that the time spent in data entry and computer programming was more than regained by avoiding lengthy manual recalculations.[1]

Based on the above information, plot each shelf title by title, and include those shelves to be left empty for growth. It is useful to have a complete diagram of each stack side such as the one shown in figure 5-2.

The form should have spaces large enough to write in comfortably. Adapt the form to the particular needs of the library, adding as many columns as there are actual stacks per row and as many rows as there are shelves per stack. If, for example, a row contains ten stacks, make the drawing ten columns wide. If each stack contains eight shelves, make the drawing eight spaces high.

Starting with the first stack, assign each row a letter of the alphabet. Figure 5-2, for example, might represent row A, stacks 1 through 5. The back side of the same stack would be row B, stacks 1 through 5. Assign letters and numbers in order, following the alphabetical arrangement in which titles will be placed, snaking back and forth around the stacks, always working from left to right.

---

[1] Brogan, Linda L. and Carolyn E. Lipscomb. "Moving the Collections of an Academic Health Sciences Library" *Bulletin of the Medical Library Association* 70 (1982): 374-379.

(fig. 5-2)

After the correct information is gathered on the 3 x 5 cards (fig. 5-1), it can easily be transferred to the diagram in figure 5-2. Make the drawing in such a scale as to allow room for each title on the shelf to be written in the appropriate square. (A computer spreadsheet program is a handy device for drawing up the prototype of the form.) After all the appropriate information is plotted onto the form, it will reveal which shelf/shelves each title will occupy in the new library. For example, *The Journal of Philosophy* may appear on row Q, stack 3, shelves 1-3 while shelf four is left for expansion. *Harper's,* a closed entry, occupies row M, stacks 5,6, and 7, with no empty shelves.

Using this as a guideline, determine how many shelves each title will occupy. Generate an auto-adhesive label for each shelf (or more than one per shelf if several titles will be placed there). A word processor can produce such labels easily and cheaply. Large libraries which do not have access to their own word processing equipment might find it worthwhile to contract the production of labels to a third party. Often there is someone in the organization or in the *Friends of the Library* group with access to a word processor who will donate the time to produce the labels if the library will purchase the supplies.

After the labels are prepared, place a label on each shelf in the new location with the title(s) of the magazine that will occupy that shelf. Place the label at the leftmost point where a given title will begin on the shelf. If *Life* and *Look* are on the same shelf, for example, the label for *Life* (at least, the final part of its run) will start at the extreme left edge of the shelf. The label for *Look* may be 22 inches from the left side. This means, then, that the first volume in the run of *Look* will be placed directly above the label-- 22 inches from the left side--and succeeding volumes will be placed in order to the right of that volume.

If the periodical volumes are to be boxed for the move, label shelves at the old location according to the location the volumes will occupy in the new library. *The Journal of Philosophy* would have a label under the first volume reading Q-3-1. Whichever volume occurs 36" later would have a label under it reading Q-3-2. Then, Q-3-3, etc. These numbers will be written on top of the boxes on moving day to inform the movers where to deliver them. The box marked Q-3-1 (and containing *The Journal of Philosophy*) will be taken to row Q, stack 3, shelf 1. Thus, boxes can be moved out of sequence and they will still arrive at the proper location. Movers will not have to waste time worrying about alphabetical order of the titles--such as whether *Journal of the American Chemical Society* should come before or after *Journal of Experimental Physiology*.

While bound periodicals are the most exacting part of the collection to be moved, proper planning will simplify the task. Doing the hard part on paper is easier than straining one's back.

CHAPTER 6

Cleaning

Because the collection will be physically shifted for the move, there are a number of tangential processes which some libraries choose to perform at this time. One of these processes is the cleaning of the materials.

Any librarian can testify that it does not take long for books on the shelf to become dusty and dirty. In one library, Friday afternoons are dedicated to evaluating used books that have been donated for the collection during the week. Because often the dust must literally be blown off the books--which have usually come from someone else's library (or basement)--before processing, Fridays are affectionately referred to as "dirty book day"--the day the librarians spend their time reading dirty books.

Since, during the move each book must be handled, some librarians feel that moving time is a self-made opportunity to clean the books also. Because the collection is probably being moved into a brand new, theoretically clean building, such a consideration at this time is wise.

In deciding whether or not to clean the collection at moving time, give first consideration to the time constraints of the move. Any additional process which is to be undertaken will slow down the move substantially.

The rationale that each book is being handled anyway is somewhat false. While it is true that each book is being moved, books do not receive individual handling but are moved in groups. While a stack of books being moved may be only eight or nine inches high, this process is still eight or nine times faster than moving them one by one. Many books are moved from one library to the other literally without ever being touched by human hands.

Adding an additional process such as cleaning will also add to the cost of the move. Increasing costs may not be wise at a time when

---

the library must bear the expense of the move itself as well as the construction costs for the new or renovated facility.

If, however, the library does decide to clean the books, combining the process with the move, may help cut costs because the materials will need to be handled only once for the two processes. In handling the two processes separately, the materials need to be transferred from point A (the stacks) to point B (the cleaning facility) and returned to point A. Then, for the move, they need to be moved from point A to point C (the new stacks). By combining the processes, they can be moved directly from A to B to C, thus eliminating considerable handling and time.

Whenever there is a limited amount of time in which to accomplish the move, it is probably wiser to concentrate solely on the move itself without adding any extraneous steps. If, for example, a library has only the weekend to move its 60,000 volumes to the new location so that it can be ready to give service to its patrons on Monday morning, it would probably not be a good idea to risk exceeding the time limit by adding the cleaning process to the move.

TECHNIQUES

There may be as many cleaning techniques as there are libraries. What type of cleaning technique should be employed depends upon the needs of the collection, available facilities, budget, and, of course, time constraints.

In some libraries it may be necessary to do nothing more than vacuum the books--in itself an arduous task without sufficient time and/or personnel. A decision must be made whether to vacuum the books as they are on the shelf, to remove each book individually, vacuum it, and replace it on the shelf to be moved later, or to remove each book, vacuum it, and place it directly into a packing carton or onto a booktruck for the move.

One technique that might prove advantageous is to vacuum the books on the top shelf first; then remove them from the shelf and pack them for the move. Next, the shelf itself can be removed from the stack, to allow access to the usually inaccessible tops of the books on the shelf below. Removing each shelf of books gives access to the tops--the dirtiest part--of the books on the shelf below.

Other libraries may choose to handle each book individually, going so far as to clean the covers with book cleaner and to perform whatever mending is necessary. It must be stressed, however, that such attention to detail will slow down the move considerably. A move is a time to think and act in bulk, NOT in detail.

Blowing is by far a more thorough technique than vacuuming for removing dust from books. However, unless something is done to absorb the dust thus produced, it is only going to settle elsewhere in the collection. Such a process is, therefore, best performed in a special work area outside either the new or the old library. Adequate provisions must be made for the health and safety of those conducting the operation so that they are not inhaling the dust.

For libraries with sufficient finances, there are available commercial cleaning apparatuses which clean books in bulk. One such device is a chamber into which books are placed and then cleaned with a blower hose; a huge vacuum absorbs the dust which is then blown off the books.

If the books are to be cleaned en masse, the issue becomes one of how many books can be cleaned at once. How long does it take to clean a load? Can several loads of books undergo the process simultaneously, or at least be in different stages of the process? If several steps are required, can load one undergo process A and then move on to process B while load two undergoes process A? Or is it necessary to wait for load one to move through the entire process and be shelved in the new library before beginning to unshelve load two? The final result of these calculations will give the amount of time it takes to move X number of books from point A, clean them, and move them to point B. This number times the number of volumes to be moved will tell us how long it will take to complete the entire move.

The simplest of cleaning methods is the old fashioned way-- dusting the books with a soft brush or feather duster. Again, however, we are faced with the problem that the dust is going to settle somewhere--if not in the lungs of the person doing the cleaning, then on the books which are still on the shelves. If a commercial preparation is sprayed on the duster, more of the dust will stick to it, but the problem will be that the duster needs frequent cleaning--certainly not desirable when there are many hundreds or thousands of books to be cleaned. Such a preparation may also produce a chemical reaction that will have a longterm effect on the preservation of the books.

When Goshen College (Goshen, Indiana) moved its library in 1967, the college sponsored a work party to clean the *new* library on the night before the move. Since a lot of dust had been left by the construction crews, such an effort was felt necessary. All friends of the college were invited to participate. Dusting cloths were provided, but each person was to bring his or her own vacuum cleaner, rags, and bucket. The college served refreshments to the participants. Such an idea might also be useful for cleaning the books in the old library.

The idea of cleaning the books before or during a move should not be passed over lightly, for the advantages are obvious: Cleaning prolongs the life of the materials, and cleaning before taking the materials to the new location reduces the amount of dirt there will be to damage books in that location. However, each library must evaluate its needs and its resources in terms of time constraints, manpower, and finances, and make the decision which is most appropriate for its situation.

CHAPTER 7

Fumigation

Another tangential process to which libraries often give consideration during or shortly before a move is that of fumigation.

As with any related operation, first consideration must be given to the time constraints of the move. If time is at a premium, concentrate solely on the move. Adding any additional process, no matter how desirable it may seem, will only bog things down.

Why fumigate? The answer is somewhat obvious: to avoid carrying vermin from the old building to the new. But, the question goes beyond that.

How big a problem are vermin in the present location? What type of vermin? Rodents? If books are going to be removed from the stacks, placed immediately in boxes or on trucks and immediately moved to the new location, it will likely be difficult for rats or mice to hitch a ride, even without fumigation. If, on the other hand, the materials being moved include boxed materials or stuffed furniture where rodents could conceivably be nesting and therein be transferred to the new location, serious consideration should be given to fumigation.

Insects? What type? Is there evidence of infestation? Can you be sure that the damage done to the materials was done by vermin still living, or could it have been done before the materials (specifically used gift books) were added to the collection and the perpetrators are no longer present? At this point, it is best to call in an expert.

Professional exterminators are experts who know how to recognize infestation and to treat it. But, how much damage is caused to library materials by the toxins professional exterminators use is a hotly debated issue. (It is somewhat like the issue of installing sprinkler systems in libraries: Will the fire cause more damage than the resulting flood?) Will the chemicals used for extermination cause more damage to the materials in terms of deterioration than the voracious appetites of the little beasties themselves? Both sides continue to argue their cases vociferously.

There are, within the library field, those who specialize in extermination of vermin among library materials. Their services are not inexpensive, so, again, each library must examine the value of such services as opposed to their cost. Providers can often be located through the classified section which appears near the end of many professional library journals.

Extermination is not a do-it-yourself project. Once the need has been established, it is time to call in an expert.

In conjunction with the expert, a determination must be made as to what type of extermination is necessary. In some cases a general fumigation may be sufficient. At other times, a more complete extermination may be necessary.

In the case of a general fumigation, it might only be necessary to close the library for a day or two while the exterminators "fog" the building--much as they would do in a private home. Handling the books would not be necessary, and it might be possible to perform the operation on a weekend or at night when the library is otherwise closed anyway.

It must be emphasized that some people are sensitive to the toxins that remain even after the building has been declared "safe" for occupancy. Does the library cater to small children? They are often more sensitive than an adult. Are there animals in the library which may be sensitive to the chemicals? Animals? In a library? Don't forget the aquarium. Or the library cats, Baker and Taylor. Pets are often more sensitive than humans to chemical residues.

Some types of insect pests are effectively exterminated only by treating each piece of material (yes, each book) individually. Some processes require that a special solution be injected into the spine of each book in order for the treatment to kill any insects and their larvae. Such an extensive process is naturally going to generate considerable expense--not to mention that it will be extremely slow.

If this process is performed, as it will involve the handling of each book, it may be simplest after treatment just to place the treated books into boxes for their transfer to the new location. Are those members of the moving crew who will be handling the materials sensitive to the effects of the chemicals used in the treatment? Or will the fumigators themselves place the materials into boxes, thereby saving the library the expense of hiring a crew to pack the books? Will the fumigators charge extra for doing so? How much?

If it is resolved to perform this process, the remaining question to be asked is how long will it take to get each and every book fumigated and into the moving boxes? Add to this the length of time necessary to move and reshelve the materials, and it is possible to determine how long it will take to move the collection to the new library.

Again, as fumigation is an issue requiring professional expertise, the library must decide whether to risk potential damage to the materials by hiring a general purpose--and probably local-- exterminator or to withstand the expense of bringing in a specialist in library fumigation--probably from some distance away. Based on the cost and time estimates provided by the fumigator, the library can decide whether or not to have the job performed at moving time.

CHAPTER 8

Deacidification

Deacidification is a process which has been much discussed in the professional library literature in the last few years, particularly as many librarians are becoming more conscious of the need to make a deliberate effort toward the preservation of materials. They are seeing many valuable and irreplaceable manuscripts literally turning to dust.

One of the steps in an active preservation program is the deacidification of materials. Four primary things must be pointed out regarding deacidification:

1) It is not a do-it-yourself process. Some of the methods involve dangerous chemicals and require special expertise in their application. They also require, in most cases, very expensive specialized equipment.

2) Deacidification will stop deterioration but it will not restore damage which has already been done.

3) As deacidification is not inexpensive, a general application to all library materials is probably not cost-effective. Normally, it is applied only to those materials which have been and/or will be a part of the collection for a long time, specifically those materials which have some historical or research value. The process, therefore, will be of greater value to the large academic or research library than to the small public or school library, and perhaps to the college library for selected portions of its collection.

4) Studies have shown that paper loses approximately 50% of its strength during the first seven years of its life. Therefore, some librarians stress the importance of deacidifying new materials as they are added to the collection.

On the other hand, because it is a time-consuming task to sort the collection and determine which volumes need to be treated and which do not, the end cost for treating part of the collection may be higher than that for treating the entire collection.

Ironically, it is not the very old books which are falling apart. Books which were published up until the nineteenth century were published on 100% rag paper. But around 1820 manufacturers discovered that paper could be made more cheaply from wood pulp than from cloth. Because of its high acid content due to sizing with alum rosin, paper made from wood pulp literally begins to eat holes in itself after a few decades. Modern papers often have a great number of chemical additives which result in a high acid content. According to Joyce M. Banks, Conservation and Rare Book Librarian at the National Library of Canada, "Inherent acidity is responsible for eighty-five to ninety percent of destruction in book papers, causing them to lose an estimated fifty percent of their fold strength every 7.5 years, which weakens them and ultimately reduces them to a state of embrittlement at which they break at a touch."[1]   Thus, many books published in the last one hundred years are virtually destroying themselves.

Anything that can be done to reduce the acid content of its pages will lengthen the life of a book. A simple washing with water will remove a great deal of acidity, though it adds no preservatives to assure continued strength. Up until just a few years ago, aqueous--water-based--deacidification processes were the only ones available. However, because the application of water tends to cause paper to wrinkle, new alternatives were sought.

---

[1]Banks, Joyce M. "Mass Deacidification at the National Library of Canada" *Conservation Administration News* no. 20

About ten years ago, it was discovered that there are ways to deacidify materials using a nonaqueous solution. Today, there are still very few nonaqueous deacidification processes available. Two of them have virtually eclipsed the others, and there is constant debate in the literature over which of the two is better.

DEZ

The Diethyl Zinc or DEZ process is currently under development by the Library of Congress to deacidify its own collection. A special facility was built by the Library of Congress at a cost of some $11.5 million which will deacidify approximately 500,000 volumes a year, at an estimated average cost in the range of three to four dollars per book[2]   The process has been fraught with problems. Diethyl zinc is highly flammable upon contact with air and explodes upon contact with water, and there have been accidents at the LC facility. After two fires, NASA ordered the building demolished in early 1986. Because of the inherent danger involved in using diethyl zinc, it must be used at a specialized facility away from the library. The Library of Congress facility is located at Ft. Detrick, Maryland, approximately 50 miles away from the Library of Congress. Thus, an additional logistic and economic concern in the deacidification process is the transport of the materials to and from the treatment site.

Currently, the method has still not emerged from the experimental stages and LC has given no indication of when, if ever, the process will be made available to others. Conservative estimates indicate that the LC facility will be unable to process any materials but its own for at least the next twenty years.[3]

---

[2] Smith, Richard D. "Mass Deacidification" *C&RL News* 45 (December 1984): 592

[3] Nelson, W. Dale. "Deacidification Priorities" *Wilson Library Bulletin* 59 (April 1985): 535.

WEI T'O

The Wei T'o system for mass deacidification began as research conducted by Richard D. Smith for his dissertation at the Graduate Library School of the University of Chicago from 1964 to 1970. The process has since been refined and updated.

Smith discovered a way to reduce the acid (positive hydrogen) content of paper by a process of nonaqueous deacidification. He named the process Wei T'o after an ancient Chinese god said to "protect books against destruction from fire, worms and insects, and robbers, big or small." Smith claims that his process is cheaper than that of the Library of Congress and also much safer. The actual cost has been shown to be $3.27 per book. By re-using recovered solvents, a process expected to begin in 1987, the unit cost will be reduced to approximately $2.50.

He also claims that it does a much more thorough job of strengthening books and preventing further deterioration than the DEZ method. A well-publicized test of 5000 books by LC estimated that only 50% to 55% of the books achieved the desired results.

There are actually two methods of application of Smith's nonaqueous process. The first is exclusively the domain of those with large collections. It is currently in use at the National Library and Public Archives of Canada, the British Library, and the Bibliotheque Nationale in France. The process operates like this:

The books, delivered by the National Library [of Canada] staff on booktrucks, are double-checked for suitability for deacidification while being placed in baskets prior to vacuum drying. The baskets of bone-dry books are loaded, two baskets at a time, into the pressure chamber for the fifty-minute deacidification cycle. The liquified gas solution is forced into the books. Then they are vacuum dried to remove the liquified gas solvent and deposit the deacidification agent throughout each book. At the end of the cycle, the baskets of books are placed inside boxes overnight to return to room conditions. Then they are inspected and returned to the

Library.[4]   A facility operating at full capacity can process about 5000 books in 24 hours.[5] The equipment is available from Wei T'o Associates who will perform the on-site installation and monitor the treatment process.

The second method, called the "Soft Spray" method, is far more cost-effective for those wishing to deacidify a small collection or a small portion of their collection. It consists of two primary pieces of equipment, both available for purchase from Wei T'o Associates. The first is a pressure sprayer (similar to a cylinder of propane gas). The pressurized tank contains the deacidification solution. The other piece of equipment is a table-top-size aluminum frame which serves both to hold the material being treated and as an exhaust fan to draw off the excess spray solution. The book to be treated is placed on the rack with the front cover open. It is then lightly but thoroughly sprayed with the deacidification solution. The method is time consuming in that each two-page spread be sprayed separately from the front of the book to the back. Thus, a one hundred page book would need to be sprayed fifty times. Though the spray process goes quickly, obviously it is satisfactory only for a very small collection.

Smith himself feels that the time-consuming deacidification process is totally incompatible with the constraints of moving a collection and, except for the most special of circumstances, should not even be considered during the moving process.[6]

Those libraries considering adding deacidification as a part of their moving process should remember that the process is expensive

---

[4] Smith, Richard D. "Mass Deacidification: The Wei T'o Understanding" *C&RL News* 48 (January 1987): 7.

[5] Smith, Richard D. "Mass Deacidification" *C&RL News* December 1984): 592.

[6] Smith, Richard D. Conversation with the author. January 20, 1987.

and time-consuming. If they wish to treat only part of their collection--which, indeed, may be preferable--it will mean sorting the collection and handling volumes individually. In any case, they should be sure to contact a commercial vendor offering deacidification services well in advance of the move.

CHAPTER 9

Setting the date.

Many otherwise well-planned moves have failed miserably because enough care was not exercised in choosing the date. If everything is set for the big day and a ground blizzard with zero visibility and wind chills in the minus 30s moves in, even the most carefully planned move will probably have to be postponed. If an alternate plan of action has not been formulated, it can spell disaster.

It must be remembered in planning any move to have an alternate plan and alternate dates available. Leave as many options as possible. If it rains on Wednesday--Moving Day--it might just as easily rain again on Thursday--the scheduled Rain Date. What will happen if it does? What if a winter blizzard moves in? Can the move be postponed to the following week? Can it be postponed for another two weeks? The move director who has allowed himself the greatest number of options regarding the move date will have the greatest chance of a successful move.

THE WEATHER.

The first and most obvious variable to consider in scheduling a move is the weather. Though some locations have an obvious advantage, such as a regular rainy or dry season, the weather is probably the most difficult factor to predict in trying to set a move date. Because the weather cannot be predicted with any degree of reliability more than a day or two ahead of time--and sometimes not even then--alternate plans must be made to allow for inclement weather.

If it should rain on move day, would postponement be the best solution? If 500 alumni have returned to campus to help carry the books, postponement might be counter productive. What is an acceptable alternative to postponement?

When Taylor University of Upland, Indiana, moved their collection of 150,000 volumes a distance of several hundred yards to the new library, it turned out to be the only rainy day for a week either side of the move. Dozens of alumni and friends of the college had shown up to help. Three television stations and several newspapers had reporters standing by to cover the event. The president of the university had allowed classes to be cancelled for the day so students could help with the move. To postpone the move and return the students to class would have been counter-productive; few would have been able (or willing) to concentrate on their studies.

It not only rained on moving day, it poured non-stop for almost twenty-four hours. Yet, postponement would have been impractical. About 8 a.m. the decision was made to go ahead; move time was scheduled for 10 o'clock.

To protect the workers and the materials, three-person teams were stationed just inside each exit from the old library. The first person took the books from the exiting volunteer. The second person poked a hole in a large dry-cleaner-size plastic bag and shoved it down over the volunteer's head and body in the form of a poncho. Once inside the bag, the volunteer poked two holes for his arms. Then, he once again got his books from the first person and advanced a few steps. The third team member shoved a small plastic bag over the library materials and the volunteer's hands. Thus, the workers and the materials were protected from the rain very quickly and efficiently without having to step out of line, put their materials on a table somewhere, get dressed, pick up the materials and struggle to cover them.

Because someone had the foresight to have ready a supply of plastic bags of the appropriate sizes, the move was able to continue as planned with a minimum of inconvenience.

BEATING THE SEASONS.

In some areas of the world, planning the weather is not so much a factor as beating the seasons. Those in cold climates, for example, may want to plan a move in the early fall before snow begins to fly. Even if the weather is beautiful outside, wet snow tracked in on a brand new beige carpet can leave irreparable damage--especially if the snow is full of substances applied to help remove it, such as salt or cinders. And cold drafts from keeping the building doors open while books are loaded or unloaded can create hours of misery for those working in nearby offices.

Sometimes rather than rushing a move to beat bad weather, it should be postponed until the season for bad weather is past. A library in Michigan, for example, might decide that a move in May would be better than one in March. Don't permit the move to be locked into a time schedule forcing it to beat a certain completion date. To do so is to potentially doom oneself to failure.

THE FINISHED BUILDING.

At all costs, unless there is some otherwise greatly restraining factor, the move director and the library director should get their superiors to agree that the move will not take place until the building has been completely and officially handed over to the institution by the construction firm. The reasons for taking such a dogmatic stance are legion.

The most obvious reason is that even though the collection be in place after the move, an unfinished building might not be ready for service to its public--or its staff. Restrooms might not be available yet. There might be no drinking water in the building. Or any water at all for processing materials and cleaning up. Or any heat, or electricity. It might be dangerous to have a construction crew hanging the ceiling over the heads of the staff. It's difficult to keep one eye on the typewriter and the other on the ceiling. A dropped ceiling might turn out to be just that.

Has the carpeting been laid and the lighting installed? These are but two of the tasks which must be completed before the stacks can be assembled. As stacks are usually installed on top of the carpet, it will be impossible to install them until the carpet is laid. If the assembled stacks are in the way, it may be impossible to set up ladders to install the lighting. Therefore, because each step must take place in a proscribed order, if the carpeting gets delayed or the light fixtures are shipped to Shipshewana, the move date may have to be postponed. It is wise not even to set a firm move date until the building has been completed. The delay of a single step in the construction process can produce a domino effect, throwing the entire completion off schedule. The Utah State University Library can confirm this experience.[1] Their library was scheduled to open to the public on January 6, 1964. Yet, many pieces of equipment did not arrive until late January.

Liability regulations might prohibit a building from being occupied while construction is underway, resulting in many days or weeks when the public would not be allowed to enter the new building. If staff were not allowed to enter, it could result in a loss of productivity at great expense to the institution (though the staff might welcome an unscheduled holiday).

Another reason for not accepting an unfinished building is to avoid legal loopholes. If the contractor is bound to hand over the building by a certain date or pay a penalty, he may leave certain details unfinished in order to beat the deadline. If the library accepts those conditions by occupying the building, the contractor may be relieved of whatever penalty there might be, and the unfinished details may remain forever unfinished. In some cases that penalty may be the only "clout" the library has; don't be eager to relinquish it.

There may also be flaws in the finished building which would not be apparent were the move to take place before completion of the

---

[1]Chappell, D. LaMont. "Operation Move" *Utah Libraries* 7 (Spring, 1964): 7-8+.

structure; if the building is occupied, they might be easily hidden behind or among the furnishings and not be discovered until it is too late for recourse.

On the other hand, if the building is occupied before completion, thereby releasing the contractor of liability, mistakes might be committed by the building crew in the final stages of construction-- after the move. If the contractor has been relieved of liability, he is, in essence, given a free hand to commit whatever atrocities his conscience will bear. More than one library has moved into a brand new uninspected structure only to discover that the roof of the new library leaks as badly as the roof of the old one.

A pre-move inspection of the *finished* building provides an opportunity to detect and remediate those flaws.

Is the lighting going to be adequate in an area which will have stacks soaring to 90 inches from the floor? What looks acceptable to the architect on his blueprint may be judged inappropriate by the trained eye of the professional librarian. The author knows of one multi-million-dollar library in which the hanging light fixtures cleared the tops of the stacks by a scant two inches. Though a major remodeling was avoided--barely--the lighting, with its many strange shadows, is woefully inadequate; unfortunately, the new building was accepted and occupied before it was completed.

Even if the flaws are detected and the contractor agrees to fix them, it just might not be possible once the building is occupied. In the example just cited, even if the architect agreed to replace the existing lighting with something more appropriate, it would be practically impossible because the stacks are in the way.

On the tour of inspection, check for details before accepting the building. Visualize the completed, functioning library as it should appear after the move. Are the electrical outlets placed near desk locations where they are supposed to be according to the blueprints? Has the appropriate type of thermostat been installed so the system can be changed from heating to cooling at the flick of a switch without necessitating a work order to the maintenance crew? Has the appropriate type of lock been installed on each window? Was the promised alarm system placed on each door and is it working?

If things are not as they should be, delaying the move until after seeing the finished building will allow for changes--either by the architect or by the librarian. Can desks be shifted around conveniently enough to avoid the delay of installing additional outlets? If there are dark aisles in the stack area, would it be better to run the stacks north and south rather than east and west? It's much easier to move them on paper now than it will be to wait until they're actually in place and filled with books. Is the building properly secure? It would be a major mistake to move millions of dollars-worth of books into a location which cannot be properly secured the first night after the move. Have the construction cores in the locks been replaced with cores that conform to the system used by the institution so that the library director can get in and out? What if the moving crew shows up for work and no one can open the new library?

The list of details is endless, but it is of utmost importance that the finished building be examined by the trained eye of a professional librarian--one who will live and work in the building--before it is accepted. The professional librarian will see things that would never occur to the business officer or the president of the college. In fact, ample opportunity should be provided for everyone who is to form part of the library staff, professional and paraprofessional, to examine the new building, especially his or her own workspace, and report back to the library director in full detail.

The building should not be accepted without final approval from the library director. It cannot be overemphasized that the moving date definitely should not be set until the building has been accepted. No matter how constraining other factors might seem at the time, the library which moves prematurely may spend the next thirty years paying for its mistake.

If the unfortunate decision is made for the move to take place before the building is completed, the move director must determine whether construction workers will be present on move day(s). If so, there are many additional problems that must be faced. In moving the Joseph Regenstein Library at the University of Chicago, Robert Moran noted that one of the problems was at the delivery

area[2] If construction crews are tying up the loading dock by
unloading materials necessary for the construction of the building,
how long will the moving crew have to stand idle until the area
becomes available to them?

Another problem Moran noted was the lack of staging areas. A
staging area is an area near the delivery entrance in which full boxes
or booktrucks can be stacked and left until workers are able to take
them to the stacks or in which empty boxes or booktrucks can be
stacked until the truck arrives to load them for the return trip. As
boxes or booktrucks can be unloaded from a truck much more
quickly than moving crews can disperse them, there will be a
bottleneck in the delivery area each time a truck arrives. If
construction crews are taking up valuable floor space for their
equipment which is not yet installed, the all-important staging areas
will be at a premium.

If construction workers will be present on move day, will
movers and construction workers be in each other's way? Things
are likely to get quite crowded and each crew is likely to think that
its job is the most important, that it has priority for the space.
Tempers may flare--a situation that should be avoided when
everyone is already working under a maximum of pressure.

There seems to be general agreement in the literature supporting
this author's experience that any move should be postponed until the
building is completed. After moving the Tulane University Library
to its Howard-Tilton Memorial building, John Gribbin states that
one of the lessons learned is "if at all possible, do not move into a
new library building until construction is entirely completed.
Confusion and conflict will result if this recommendation is not
followed."[3]

[2]Moran, Robert F., jr. "Moving a Large Library" *Special
Libraries* 63 no. 4 (April 1972): 163-171.

[3]Gribbin, John H. "Tulane Library Moves Across the Street"
Louisiana Library Association Bulletin 32 (Spring 1969): 26-30.

AVAILABILITY OF WORKERS.

A move cannot be accomplished without workers and it, therefore, depends entirely upon their availability. Though we have not yet discussed the matter of determining the method of moving, obviously, the method must be determined before considering the availability of workers.

A move with professional help will, in part, be determined by the availability of the movers. In negotiating with them, several alternate dates should be suggested which are mutually acceptable to both parties. If the professional company is too rigid in selecting a date for the move, perhaps it would be wise to consider a different company altogether. A good company will try to work with the library and remain as flexible as possible. Such a company may also offer alternatives should the move have to be postponed.

Whether paid workers or volunteers are used, the move director must examine their availability. Are they students on vacation whose schedule has a great deal of flexibility? Do the workers hold jobs elsewhere from which they are taking time off to help with the move? If the move is postponed, will they be unavailable or will they lose an extra day's pay? Are the workers returning alumni or *Friends of the Library* who have traveled to this location at great expense to themselves (or to the library)? If they must stay over, can they arrange overnight accommodations conveniently? Are there library personnel available to assist in making such arrangements? For a college library, have classes been cancelled at the institution or, in the case of a public library, perhaps at a nearby college, to allow students to help in the move? What will they do if the move is postponed? Will they be available later?

If the movers are student volunteers from the college where the library is located, is it important to finish the move before students leave campus for the summer?

If only the library staff is going to be involved in the move, perhaps there is a greater deal of flexibility in determining the move date, since staff is obviously going to be there working for the library every day anyway.

NEED TO EVACUATE OLD FACILITY.

In cases in which the library is moving to a totally new facility, the move may be pushed along by those riding on its tail. What is to become of the old building? Is it going to be remodeled into office space? Has the owner promised the space to new clients by a certain deadline? How much flexibility is there in vacating the facility? Is there an absolute deadline by which the premises must be vacated? What are the possible consequences if that deadline is not met?

The library director and the move director should enter into negotiations as early as possible with the owner of the old location in determining the exit date. The owner may often be a third party or, perhaps, another branch of the institution of which the library itself is a member--such as the city government in the case of a public library, or the college in the case of an academic library. Often it is easier to negotiate with a third party than with another branch of one's own institution.

If the library is directly responsible for the old building, what is to become of it? Is it going to be sold? Is there a deadline for the sale? Must it be remodeled by a certain date prior to the sale? Or is it going to be turned into book storage or a branch, in which case there might not be such a rush to vacate?

The move director must be open to negotiation with the parties involved and must be of strong enough character to be able to say when necessary, "We cannot move by that date. We will NOT move by that date."

NEED TO PROVIDE SERVICE.

Before the date can be set for any move, it must be determined by when and under what circumstances service must be provided in the new location.

From the standpoint of making a convenient and efficient move, it is probably best to close the library completely during a move. Such a decision, however, may not always be possible. Some libraries are obligated to provide continuing service, even during the move. The library director must first determine whether service may be suspended and for how long.

When Princeton University moved into the Harvey S. Firestone Building in 1948, the move was planned during the university summer session. It was decided to continue library services without interruption. The move was structured so that no book would be out of circulation for more than three or four hours.[4]

If service must continue, how can this best be accomplished? Is it necessary to provide full service or only partial service? Can some services be moved to the new location while others continue to be offered temporarily from the old location?

Must some services be suspended for the time being? A public library, for example, might decide that it is able to continue all services except children's storyhour because of the traffic created by the move and the safety of the children involved. Another library might see that it is impossible to keep its doors open to the public but may continue to provide telephone reference service. Or, inversely, due to the number of staff tied up with the move, a library might be open for circulation but suspend all other services involving a drain on personnel time.

The library director must work closely with the move director in determining which services are to be moved and when. The move director must take into account which staff members will be busy offering service to the public and when and thus not be available to assist in the move. The move director must also decide how best to move the other services with the least interruption in the ongoing services.

---

[4]"Princeton University Moves Into Its New Building" *Library Journal* 73 (September 1, 1948): 1210-1212.

DAY OR NIGHT.

While a case hardly need be made for the advantages of carrying out a move during daylight hours, such a timeframe is not always possible or practical. Some moves are best made at night or on weekends.

In cases in which a library must provide ongoing service to its users, night or weekends might be the only times a move can be carried out. Even if daylight is an option, the hours during which the library is closed to the public might offer the greatest convenience

Several years ago one library in a major metropolis decided that night was the most effective time for the move because loaded booktrucks had to be wheeled across a busy downtown thoroughfare. Crossing the street was much easier during the lightly travelled hours of the night than in bustling daytime traffic.

If, on the other hand, the move is to be carried out at night, several additional variables enter the scene. Is personnel available at night? It might be possible to keep the library staff or a crew of volunteers from their sleep for a night, but can it be done for several nights? It is certainly unfair to expect the library staff to work their full shift during the day and then spend the night hours helping move the library.

Will the lack of daylight cause the need for additional lighting? Are light fixtures already installed in the necessary locations, or will installation be necessary? Who will foot the bill for the installation? If the answer is "the library," is there funding available in the budget?

Are there some difficult areas that just cannot be lighted under any circumstances? How much problem is that likely to cause?

Is security an issue? Since many public libraries are in downtown urban areas, there may be a criminal element on the streets at night. A library cannot expect its workers to place themselves in a position in which they might be mugged or harmed bodily without providing adequate security. Can the library provide *adequate* security? Is the cost of providing such security reasonable enough to offset the expenses of carrying out the move during daylight hours?

In planning a night move, the move director should examine the moving route at night. It is not sufficient to evaluate the move during the day and project what it will be like at night. Examine the route under circumstances as similar as possible to those expected during the actual move. In considering the lighting, remember that the same full moon of the examination may not shine upon the actual move.

In determining the date for the move, the move director must work as closely as possible with all those involved. He should make every attempt to be as flexible as possible and try to evaluate every factor. But it should be established from the beginning that the move director has the ultimate authority; his word for determining when the move shall take place is not to be overridden by the library director, the chairman of the board of trustees, the college president, the professional mover, or anyone else.

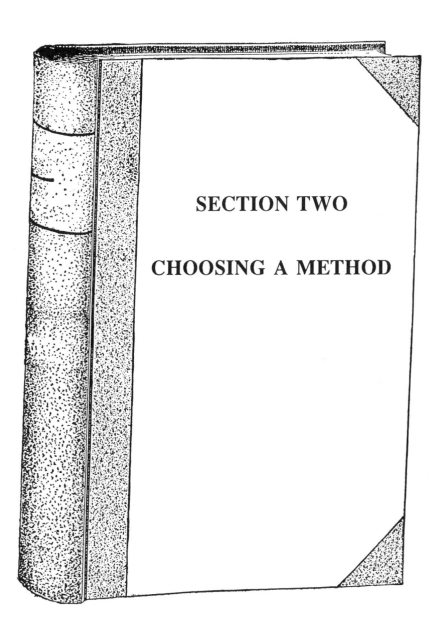

SECTION TWO

CHOOSING A METHOD

CHAPTER 10

Loose books

A method used by many libraries, particularly when the budget is tight, is that of using workers to pass loose books without containers of any type to the new location. Though there are some advantages to this method, there are also many disadvantages.

ADVANTAGES.

1) Workers need not possess any special skills other than a willing spirit and the ability for a little physical labor.

2) A great deal of training is not required. With brief explanations, workers can be oriented to the method and spend the time working rather than training.

3) There is not a great deal of overhead expense for things like vehicles, boxes or booktrucks.

4) The method itself promotes team spirit and a feeling of camaraderie. Because workers are forced to cooperate with one another and because the method, once underway, does not require a great deal of thought or conversation, workers tend to share with each other about other subjects. They begin to function as a team and soon find themselves making new friends or enjoying old ones.

DISADVANTAGES.

1) Because the work is monotonous, workers tend to become careless after a while. Not understanding the chain reaction that mistakes can cause later, workers tend to consider them of relative unimportance. Mistakes are easily made and not always corrected.

2) As this method usually employs volunteers, those problems which are associated with any method using volunteers tend to creep in. Non-librarian volunteers don't understand the reason for doing things in a certain way and tend to cut corners.

3) Loose books are unprotected from the elements should the weather be less than perfect. Even on a sunny day, if the move is between buildings, the materials will be subjected to damaging sunlight.

4) Loose books are easy to drop, and there is nothing to protect them from damage when they are dropped.

5) Workers who do not understand call number order (or who don't care) will gather up the books from the shelf or after dropping them in random order and thus transfer the misarrangement to the shelf at the new location.

During its move in 1981, the Albany County Library of Laramie, Wyoming, discovered many of the problems of using the loose book method. "After no new books had arrived at the new library for several minutes, library director Lisa Kinney began the three block 'jog' to the old library to find a woman at the bottom of the stairs of the old library reading her favorite passage from a book to the entranced volunteers around her. Other stoppages occurred with dancing teenagers, six three-year-olds in a row, and a contest on who could pile up the most books to pass along."[1]

---

[1]Kinney, Lisa. "Albany Co. Library On the Move" *Wyoming Library Roundup* 37 (Fall 1981): 1-3.

There are basically two methods of getting loose books from one location to another.

WALKING IN LINE.

The first method is often called "walking in line." Each worker gets an armload of books from the old library and walks to the proper location in the new library while maintaining his sequence in a line of workers.

The most obvious problem--and the most frequent--is that workers often have trouble maintaining their place in the line. If, for example, the library is offering a prize to the worker who makes the most trips, the worker may skip around those in front of him in order to complete more trips. Otherwise, some people just naturally walk faster than others. Workers may walk side by side between locations so they can converse on the way and forget what order they were in by the time they reach the new library.

On one occasion, a worker was observed saying to her friend, "I've got too many books. Here, take some of mine." Whereupon she pulled several books from the top of her stack and placed them on top of her friend's stack--far removed from their proper place in the call number sequence.

If, as often happens, several groups are simultaneously pulling books from various locations in the old library, a worker could mistakenly follow the wrong line. By the time he returns to his correct line, those coming after him in the sequence may have long since shelved their books, thus placing his books far down the row of stacks from their proper place.

The work tends not to flow at an even pace between the locations. Often, there may be a delay in removing books from the old shelves because they are dropped as they are taken or because the line has reached the end of a stack and must swing around to the other side of the row or even to another location to continue the sequence. Thus, the worker may have long since lost sight of the person he is supposed to follow.

A modification that some libraries have made to the loose book method is using canvas bags. While the method will increase the cost because of the expense of the bags, it may prove to be less expensive in the long run because of the decrease in wear and tear on books. The book bags provide added protection to the books, no matter what the weather. They permit each worker to carry more books than is possible if they are carried loose. And the bags make it more comfortable for the workers because they provide a handhold, thus allowing the books to be carried with the arm extended rather than bent; workers will tire less quickly. A disadvantage is that the process of bagging and unbagging the books will slow down the move considerably.

Duchess Community College in Poughkeepsie, New York, used canvas book bags that measured 1 1/2 feet long by one foot deep, which they ordered from a local army surplus store.[2] Many of the supply houses from which libraries normally order their supplies have such bags in various sizes, often available with the library's logo printed on the side.

Though the bags may add to the cost of the move, they can later be used to help out at the circulation desk. When a patron checks out more books than he can comfortably carry, or when the weather is inclement, he can be lent a book bag along with the books he is borrowing. Even if there is no circulation control kept of the bags, the disappearance rate tends to be low when the library's logo is emblazoned on the side. If all such bags remain library property, anyone seeing a bag knows that it belongs to the library and should be returned.

An alternate use for the bags is as promotional items, such as door prizes at some library-sponsored event. They might even be given as souvenirs to those who helped with the move. However, if some bags are to be given away and others are to be used as mentioned in the previous paragraph, circulation records of the bags should be kept to retard their unauthorized disappearance. Or possibly, if bags are purchased in more than one color, bags of a certain color could remain library property, while others are given away.

---

[2]Feret, Barbara L. "Moving the Library at Dutchess Community College," *ALA Bulletin* 61 (January 1967): 68-71.

When using the "walking in line" method some libraries use several lines of workers pulling books from several different places in the call number sequence in order to expedite the move. Certainly, such a practice is recommendable, as it will proportionately shorten the amount of time required for the move. However, such simultaneous moving of portions of the collection will require much careful planning.

Some libraries have found it advantageous to divide the workers into teams and give each team a color code: a red team, blue team, yellow team, green team, etc. Sometimes a color is given a special meaning. For example, red might mean reference materials and periodicals so that those not wishing to carry these materials, which tend to be heavy, might join a team of another color. If book bags are used, different teams may be coded by the color of the bag they carry.

In advance of the move, lines are somehow marked on the surface of the floor, both in the new and old libraries and on the ground in between. Colored booktape, though tending to be expensive, works well on many surfaces, indoors and out. It is possible to use spray paint for lines on outdoor sidewalks. On carpeted surfaces, 10" long strips of appropriately colored construction paper held down with double-faced tape is a system that works surprisingly well; although one would expect the paper to be ruined as hundreds of pairs of feet walk over it, it lasts much longer than one would think. Except for some types of paint, most types of markers tend to become effaced and will have to be replaced occasionally during the move.

It is not necessary that the lines be continuous if, for example, the team is led onto a sidewalk which runs for a hundred feet with no crosswalks nor intersections. Only at the intersections must there be clear markings. Remember that the worker didn't plan the route, and doesn't know it and can't be expected to guess what it's supposed to be. At any location where there might be confusion the route must be plainly marked.

Thus, a worker pulling from the yellow section in the old library follows the yellow markers out of the building. There, he starts in the direction the yellow markers indicate and continues in that direction until seeing another marker. He follows the markers into the new building where he picks up new markers which lead him to the stacks where his load of books is to be deposited. From there, markers lead him out of the new library via a return route to his starting place in the old library, and the cycle is repeated.

Because the beginning and ending points of the route will shift somewhat as stacks are emptied in the old location and filled in the new, markers near the ends of the routes must be easily movable.

BUCKET BRIGADE.

The other method used for the delivery of loose books is the "bucket brigade." In this method, a human chain is formed from the location in the old building where books are being pulled to the location in which those books are to be shelved in the new building. The workers then, remain stationary, holding their place in line. Books are passed hand to hand from one end of the line to the other--from the old location to the new.

The primary consideration is the number of workers needed to stretch from the old location to the new location. The distance, and thus the number of workers needed, may vary at different times during the move. If the reference collection is to be moved from just inside the door of the old library to just inside the door of the new library, the distance may be only two hundred feet. But when the curriculum books are moved from the basement of the old library to the fourth floor of the new library, the distance might be seven hundred fifty feet. Where will the additional workers for the extra five hundred fifty feet come from? If they are available for the longer move, will they just stand around and wait while the reference collection is being moved for the shorter distance?

With this method, the most obvious problem is that it is extremely easy to drop books when passing them from one person to another. Even the most careful worker cannot avoid dropping the occasional book. Considering that books may pass through as many as several hundred pairs of hands before they reach the new location, it is a wonder that every book in the collection is not dropped at least once during the move.

In using this method, it must be determined how large a stack of books can be passed comfortably and safely at one time. It is here that the law of the chain applies: A chain is only as strong as its weakest length. No more books can be passed through the chain at one time than the amount which can be handled by its weakest member. Can the slowest, weakest worker efficiently handle one book? two books? a stack six inches high? nine inches high?

If workers can handle only one or two books at at time, how long will the move take? How long does it take a book to go from the old shelf at one end of the chain to the new shelf at the other end? How long does it take for ten books? Would another method go faster? All this must be planned and tested before time of the move and should be part of the time-and-motion study.

When one sequence has been exhausted and it is necessary to start pulling books from a new location, how difficult will it be to move the human chain around through the stacks in the library to the new location? What is the best route to take to avoid having people step on each other? Should they back out of the building and then walk from the door to the new location? Or should the chain double back on itself? Perhaps the chain should break in two at the door, be rethreaded to the new location and then rejoin the other section.

Obviously, the logistics involved in using a human chain can be mind-boggling.

The loose books method has been used with varying degrees of success (or failure) by many libraries. It must be noted that when accuracy is the goal, it is not a recommendable method. When the goal is simply to get the books to the new building where they will later be reshelved by the library staff after the rest of the stacks are assembled or after another collection is melded in, the method works well.

For this method, it is imperative that there be plenty of "supervisors." The supervisors are a hand-picked group of workers who, hopefully, can handle a little more responsibility than the "average" worker. These supervisors are thoroughly instructed in their task, which is to do nothing most of the time. Their primary function is simply to stand around and do nothing. Their responsibility is only to be there to spot and correct potential problems and to fill in as needed. The supervisors will not move a single book. If they see workers who are getting out of their place in line or who are dropping books because of carelessness, then, the supervisors intervene. Otherwise, they do nothing. In the ideal move, supervisors would have nothing to do--and they must be forewarned that they are likely to be bored and to feel useless--but they must be there, nevertheless, to handle whatever problems may arise.

It cannot be overstressed to the carriers that they are not to prove how "macho" they are by carrying a huge stack of books. There will "tend to [be] bottlenecks at the pickup point and ending point of these moving lines [of people] and especially at the depository or ending point of these lines. For this reason small handfuls of books will work better, because depositing a large armful of books is much more difficult than a small handful of books."[3]

The loose books method works well when one of the goals is to create a participative group spirit and lots of good will. If that good will is to be counter-balanced with the gnashing of teeth of the library staff who must later reshelve the books in some semblance of their call number sequence, another method is advisable.

The loose books method is hard on the materials, as great numbers of books tend to be dropped. If the collection which is to be moved is of considerable value, an alternate method is highly preferable. One must consider which would prove the greater expense for the library: the wear and tear on the materials which will have to be replaced so much sooner, or the cost of some other method.

---

[3]Yoder, Paton, Dean of Instruction, Hesston College, Hesston, Kansas. Letter to James Clemmens, Librarian, Goshen College, Goshen, Indiana. 3 August 1967.

CHAPTER 11

On booktrucks.

Using booktrucks, it is possible to move a large number of books, in order, in a single trip between locations. Books can be loaded in sequence from the old stacks directly onto the truck and unloaded, still in sequence, onto the new stacks. Booktrucks work especially well when the move is within the same library, such as after an addition or a remodeling project, or for a short move within the same building. When the move is longer, the booktruck method may prove impractical for such things as negotiating stairways when no elevators are available, narrow doorways or rough doorsills, or up or down steep ramps.

When the move is between buildings, it becomes more complex due to the varying types of ground surface which may be encountered. If the move is level and there is a hard, paved or concrete surface between the two locations, booktrucks may work quite well. If the old and new libraries are located on opposite sides of a dirt play yard, a grass soccer field, or a gravel parking lot, the trucks will probably prove highly inefficient.

For the move of 750,000 books in 1969, Tulane University constructed a ramp to connect its two buildings which were located across the street from each other. During a period of 56 days, booktrucks made 11,271 trips across the ramp. The advantage to using this method was that books had to be handled only twice-- once to load them onto the trucks and once to load them from the trucks to the new stacks.[1]

---

[1]Gribbin, John H. "Tulane Library Moves Across the Street" *Louisiana Library Association Bulletin* 32 (Spring 1969):26-31.

There are two types of booktrucks which may be used in moving:

The first type, obviously, is those booktrucks which are used daily to transport books within the library. A typical library booktruck has three shelves per side, each approximately three feet long. Filling the truck to capacity allows for about eighteen linear feet of books. With such weight on board, it would be wise to have two workers handling each truck.

Any rough surface will place tremendous strain on a fully loaded truck. As a result, some trucks, particularly those that are feeling their years, might not survive the move. Can the library afford to repair or replace them if they are damaged? If they cannot be replaced immediately, can the library perform its normal daily routine without them until such time as they can be replaced? A move to a larger library will probably result in a need for more, not fewer, booktrucks than those which were available in the old location.

Because of the problems caused by weight--greater strain and the necessity of two people to handle each truck--it might be wise to limit the number of books placed on the truck. If a predetermined number of linear feet of books, say ten feet, is to be placed on each stack in the new library, it can be established that when ten feet of books is placed on each truck it be considered full and sent on its way. Then, the shelvers in the new library know to move to a new stack for each truckload.

Many problems encountered by a ready-made library booktruck are due to the size of its wheels. A ready-made library booktruck tends to have relatively small wheels. The small wheels handle poorly on irregular surfaces. Often they snag or simply refuse to be pushed over an obstacle that a larger size wheel handles with ease.

When using ready-made booktrucks, check the route before moving day. Use a truck loaded with the maximum size load. If problems occur, find a satisfactory solution *before* move time.

Ready-made booktrucks have shelves that are made to handle the average size book. When handling oversize or quarto volumes, they may prove inadequate. This problem regularly occurs in moving collections of art books or bound periodicals.

Oversize books can be too large for the shelves of the booktruck in two dimensions. Books that are too tall might not fit on the second or third shelf of the truck because they don't clear the shelf above. When this occurs, it can sometimes be remedied by laying the book down on the spine or the fore-edge. Thick, heavy volumes should be placed on their spine only as placing them on the fore-edge places all the stress on the binding and allows the cover to tear loose from the block.

Books can also be too large for the shelf by being too wide for it. So much of the book hangs off the edge of the shelf that the volume is off balance and falls to the floor with any slight vibration--if not before. These books might better be moved on booktrucks which have shelves that are not divided in the center. On some trucks all three shelves continue across the full width of the truck; on others, only the top or bottom shelf is flat and full width. By loading from only one side of the truck, books can be pushed closer to the center until they are balanced well enough to stay on the truck. Using such a technique, particularly on a truck which has only one flat shelf, will, of course, result in more trips per truck to transport a given number of books.

To avoid some of the problems provoked by the standard ready-made booktruck or simply because there are not enough ready-made booktrucks available, some libraries make their own booktrucks.

The obvious advantage of a library-made booktruck is that it can be made to the library's own specifications. When rough surfaces are to be encountered, the trucks can be made with large wheels and with guards to keep books from falling off the side. If large books are to be transported, shelves can be made higher or deeper. If the library wants to make fewer trips with more books per trip, a larger booktruck can be constructed. If weight is a problem, trucks can be reinforced. Or if workers can't handle a heavy load of books in one trip, a number of smaller trucks can be built to make possible more trips.

When moving its library in 1971, Miami University had the problem of moving books from its old building via a cantankerous, undependable book lift and a narrow steel stairway to a new building which was three hundred yards away. They attacked the problem quite successfully with two dozen specially constructed heavy duty booktrucks "which would fit exactly into the confines of the book lift, taking full advantage of every cubic inch of space."[2]

[2]Alley, Brian. "Utility Book Truck Designed for Moving Library Collections" *Library Acquisitions: Practice and Theory* 3 no. 1 (1979):33-37.

CHAPTER 12

On trays or troughs.

In order to increase the number of books which can be moved per trip, some libraries have built specially constructed trays or troughs as an alternative to the "walking in line" or "bucket brigade" method. These troughs, usually constructed of wood, normally vary in length from three to nine feet with a handle at either end. The troughs are carried between two people.

Whether or not troughs are an advantage is open to discussion; there are a number of advantages, but there are also a number of disadvantages.

ADVANTAGES

Using a trough, naturally increases the number of linear feet of books that can be carried at one time from approximately nine inches to between three and nine feet--an increase of from four to twelve times. Thus, there should be a reduction in the amount of time needed to transport X number of books. We will examine this issue in greater depth in a few moments.

It is far less likely that books carried on troughs will be gotten out of order than those which are transported loosely. Even those walking in line are less likely to get out of order than those carrying loose books for at least three reasons: 1) Because of the longer loading time, the trough which they are to follow will be significantly ahead, not permitting the carriers to catch up and pass. 2) The carriers will probably be walking more slowly and, thus, find it harder to pass than if walking singly. 3) Because the trough is carried by two workers, if one wants to pass, the other can serve to remind him that passing is forbidden.

A major advantage of this system is the treatment the books themselves receive: It is far less likely that a book in a trough will be dropped than it is that a book being carried loose in someone's arms or being passed from person to person will be. On the other hand, because of the additional weight, if a troughful of books is dropped, it is conceivable that greater damage may occur--both to the books and the trough as well as to anyone who happens to be hit by them.

DISADVANTAGES

The first questions one must ask are, "Who are the workers? Will they be able to bear the weight of a fully loaded book trough nine feet long?" If the answer is negative or even in doubt, it is probably best to employ an alternate method.

A significant disadvantage to the trough method may be the longer time needed for loading and unloading the shelves. Time must be measured carefully to determine which method is faster, loose books or troughs.

It is not sufficient measure to say that it takes X minutes to get book ABC from shelf A1-old to shelf A1-new. What, in fact, must be measured is the time it takes the carriers to begin loading a trough of books at location A1-old, transport them to A1-new, unload them, and return to point B1-old, ready for the next load of books. This length of time must then be multiplied by the two because it is taking X minutes of the time of two workers, and divided by the number of books thus transported. Thus:

20 minutes x two workers = 40 work-minutes
40 work minutes / 100 books = .40 minutes (24 seconds) per book

If a worker carrying loose books can make the trip in five minutes and deliver 10 books, the formula appears thus:

5 minutes / 10 books = .5 minutes (30 seconds) per book

While, according to the above figures--which are purely conjectural--it may appear that the work would go faster using troughs, the amount of time saved must be balanced against the expense and the amount of time spent constructing the troughs.

Perhaps the most significant slow-down using the trough method is at the points of loading and unloading. A person walking singly can grab nine inches worth of books--an optimum number--by himself, walk to the new location, and shelve the books by himself. With a trough, however, those holding the ends have, at best, one hand free. It is not possible, or at least practical, to shelve and unshelve books with only one hand--as anyone who has tried it can testify; to do so takes a tremendously long time and produces a great number of dropped books, which must then be sorted and placed in the proper order. Thus, two additional people are necessary, one to place the books in the trough and another to remove the books and shelve them. As a result, the above figures are somewhat misleading, since we are now talking about the time of four, not two, people.

The time of the loader and unloader must be measured somewhat differently: Whatever time it takes them to load or unload a trough must be added to the time of the two carriers.

Another disadvantage of using troughs is the physical maneuverability. Any time the move leaves level ground, the practicality of troughs decreases. On a stairway, particularly with a long trough, one end of the trough can be significantly higher than the other, thus causing the books to shift and, perhaps, fall.

A long trough is especially difficult to maneuver through doorways and around corners. In some cases, it may be impossible to get a trough greater than a certain length around a given corner. This possibility should be given careful consideration and measurements should be taken carefully to avoid discovering such a problem on moving day.

Because of the increased weight in carrying a larger number of books, it is to be expected that workers will tire more often and will need to take breaks more frequently. Break times must be figured as part of the time necessary in transporting books from point A to point B. Again, it should be remembered that these break times are now for two people.

The amount of muscle strain produced by carrying such an amount of weight will depend somewhat upon the construction of the troughs, but, at best, the physical position a carrier must assume to grasp the handles of a trough and walk is likely to produce more backstrain than walking singly with an armload of books. The result will be an increase in the number of rest breaks or, perhaps, a decrease in the total number of trips per worker.

Because of their particular construction, most troughs are difficult to put down when they are loaded with books. If workers caught in a "traffic jam" at some point must simply stand and wait for a time, they may be forced to stand and hold the trough because of the impracticality of placing it on the ground, thus producing additional fatigue. If the trough is so constructed that it may be placed on the ground, the considerable effort required to bend low enough to put it down or pick it up may produce strained back muscles.

Another disadvantage of the trough method may be the construction of the troughs. Is there someone available who can construct them? Is there sufficient time to have them built before moving day? What will be the total cost of building them? What will happen to them after moving day? Will they be discarded? If not, will they ever be used again? Can they be sold? Is there room to store them?

In some cases the book trough method may prove advantageous over other alternatives, but each library must make a careful time-and-motion study and consider the cost in order to make that determination.

CHAPTER 13

Boxes.

Using boxes--by which we mean primarily, cardboard cartons-- to move books offers many advantages over other methods. Boxes afford the books a degree of protection from the elements. If it is necessary to move the collection during a snowstorm or when snow is on the ground, provided the snow is brushed off and not allowed to melt on the boxes after they are moved to the warm indoors, boxes provide ample protection from the snow. Even in the rain, if not too heavy, boxes offer some protection--certainly more than the books would have if they were loose. A covered box can even protect the books from drying and fading due to exposure to the sunlight.

Boxes allow the transport of a greater number of books per trip than can be managed when they are loose. The number of books per box, naturally, depends on the size of the box, as well as the size of the books. But, in any case, one worker can handle more books conveniently within a box than in a loose stack--usually two or three times as many.

When handling books in a box, the worker is less likely to drop them. Loose books can slide against one another and be squeezed out from the middle of the stack. They then fall unprotected against the ground. Books in a box stay in their correct sequence unless roughly dropped. Even when a box is dropped, it provides quite a bit of protection from damage.

Boxes can be stacked on dollies or in motorized vehicles, allowing the transport of many boxes on each trip. The books stay in order within the boxes and the boxes stay in order on the vehicle. While it might be possible to stack thousands of loose books into the back of a truck, no one would guarantee in what order or condition they would arrive at their destination. In boxes, they can arrive in the same order and condition in which they were loaded onto the truck.

Boxes are not as expensive as other types of purchased or constructed apparatuses. A cardboard box costs only a fraction of the price of a wooden book trough which will hold the same number of books.

While in the long run a wooden crate might be cheaper than a cardboard one in that the wooden one may last for years, what value will several hundred wooden crates be to the library after the move? Cardboard is definitely cheaper and easier to dispose of after the move.

Boxes can be purchased in bulk from the manufacturer. Considering the hundreds of boxes that libraries will need for a move, the price can be reduced to only a few cents apiece.

Often a donor can be found for the boxes. St. Louis University moved into its new library using donated beer cartons from the nearby Anheuser-Busch Brewery. Surely, the free publicity and good will that Anheuser-Busch has received, and continues to receive, from the pictures of the move and all that was written about it have long ago offset the cost of that contribution. Even though there may not be a container manufacturer in the area who is willing to donate the boxes, a nearby business might be willing to purchase them in exchange for a public acknowledgement or just for the tax write-off.

Boxes come already assembled, requiring no construction. If there is any assembling to do, it is merely unfolding the flattened carton and forming it into its proper shape; anyone can do it with little or no proper training.

FACTORS TO LOOK FOR IN CHOOSING A BOX.

A box should be strong enough for the job. Get a sample and load it full of books. Have several people take turns carrying it around, picking it up, setting it down, and sliding it along a rough surface. Better yet, fill it with some weeded books and drop it a few times. Get it wet. Does the box quickly start to fall apart? If it holds up, it is strong enough to do the job.

A box should have handholds. These handholds must be strong enough not to tear out when the box is fully loaded with books and jostled. Remember that the handholds will be grabbed at and pulled on. Preferably, they should be reinforced.

The ideal box will be large enough to be able to hold the majority of sizes of books to be moved. Perhaps the oversize volumes won't fit into the box the same way the regular books will, but is there room to place a stack of oversize books in the box by turning them in the other direction? If not, is there an acceptable alternative method available for moving the oversize materials or will a larger box be required?

On the other hand, a box that is too large will allow the materials to move around inside during transport and possibly get damaged or, at least, out of order. The correct size box is neither too large nor too small.

How many books should be transported per box load? Large boxes which hold a lot of books might be too heavy for the workers to carry. Large boxes might not fit on top of the dolly if dollies are used. Boxes that are too small, by contrast, will increase the work load in that more trips must be made.

If the boxes are going to be stacked or transported en masse on some type of wheeled vehicle, motorized or otherwise, great care should be taken to acquire all boxes of the same size. Boxes of the same size will stack more easily, provide a more compact load, and make it much easier to keep them in order.

A box that has proven itself many times over to be ideal is the beer carton. Approximately one foot deep, one foot wide by one and a half feet long, its reinforced bottom and handholds give it many of the desired qualities for a moving carton. Many container manufacturers sell containers with characteristics similar to this-- sans logo.

CHAPTER 14

Using vehicles.

In any move which is outside the confines of a single building, the library should give consideration to the possibility of using vehicles. Even though the distance may be relatively short and, regardless of the moving method used, using vehicles for transporting the materials may provide a significant advantage.

Consider, for example, a library which is moving from building A to building B. The new Library B is only twenty yards east of old Library A. The books are to be moved on booktrucks. To load the booktrucks onto a vehicle would necessitate removing the books from the loading dock on the west side of Library A, loading them onto a truck, and driving to the loading dock on the east side of Library B. Following the roads would add a distance of almost a quarter mile.

Where, then, is the advantage? To move the booktrucks on the ground would mean that they must descend one flight of stairs from the main floor of the library to the ground. The elevator which is used to bring books down from the upper floors stops on the main floor, but not at the ground level. The same situation is true in Library B. By using vehicles, booktrucks can be pushed to the loading ramp of Library A, which is on the level of the main floor, and pushed directly onto a truck. In Library B, they can be unloaded onto the loading dock and wheeled directly to the proper place in the new stacks.

Or, consider the above scenario without the elevators. The chosen method of moving is in boxes instead of on booktrucks. Boxes from the upper levels can be slid down a specially constructed ramp placed outside a window directly into the back of a truck waiting at the bottom of the ramp. While this will not solve the problem of transporting books to the upper levels of the new building--new libraries are far more likely to have elevators than are the old ones--it will cut the problem in half.

Naturally, using a vehicle often involves some cost, particularly if the library does not own an appropriate vehicle. Local truck rental agencies--check the yellow pages of the telephone directory under "Truck Renting & Leasing"--have a variety of sizes which are available on a daily basis for a cost ranging from fifty to one hundred dollars.

If the library is using a professional mover, the professional will usually provide his own vehicles as part of the moving contract.

It is highly recommended that the library using vehicles use at least two. Thus, one vehicle can be at the loading ramp, keeping the loading crew busy, and the other at the unloading ramp, keeping that crew busy. With proper timing, the vehicles can circulate so that neither is kept waiting for the other to get out of its way. As the travelling distance between the two libraries increases, the number of vehicles should increase, with the timing adjusted appropriately so there is always one vehicle being loaded and one being unloaded.

CHAPTER 15

Choosing helpers.

The method of choosing workers for the library move needs to be given careful consideration for, ultimately, it is on the workers which the success or failure of the move depends. The most carefully planned move cannot succeed if the workers are not capable of handling the job.

VOLUNTEERS.

Because budgets are usually tight, many libraries choose volunteers for moving their library. There are numerous advantages to using the volunteer method:

1) The price is right. A library whose already small budget has been stretched to the limit by the cost of a new building and other expenses associated with the move may find itself unable to hire workers to complete the move. Volunteers may be the only path open to such a library.

When the constraints are not so rigid, using volunteers frees funds that would normally be spent for the move to be channeled elsewhere--perhaps to collection development, furniture, or equipment for the new library. Maybe the money will be used simply to reduce the mortgage.

2) It creates good will. Often, there are many members of the community who would love to do something for their library. Voluntary participation in the move provides them with such an opportunity. Often there are many ready and willing workers in the *Friends of the Library* group. A school or academic library has an

obvious group of possible volunteers among its faculty and student body. Some libraries have done extensive publicity in acquiring volunteers to help move. They have made an all-out recruiting effort to get alumni to return to campus to see the new library and to help with the move. Thus, even though they may have left the campus years before the new library was built, they come to feel part of it. Such feeling may inspire financial contributions toward the library at sometime in the future.

Publicly recruiting volunteers is a method of reaching those who have not participated in library activities in the past. Community members who have never set foot in the library may volunteer to help with the move just because the experience is so unusual. Perhaps in the past townspeople have felt that they were unwelcome to visit the campus of the local college or even resentful that the college was in their town. The opportunity for them to help with the library move may help break down that barrier, winning the library new esteem in local eyes.

Unfortunately, the volunteer method seems to pose more hazards than advantages:

1) Volunteers cannot be told what to do. A supervisor may *ask* a volunteer to perform a certain task, but if the volunteer refuses there is no punishment nor loss of reward. He cannot be fired. The worse that can happen to a volunteer for refusing to follow instructions is that he walk off the job because he is no longer happy enough with working conditions to want to volunteer his services; the volunteer holds all the cards: He can resign, but he can't be fired. If a volunteer is asked to leave because his work is not up to standard--telling a volunteer that his free services are not good enough is a ticklish situation in itself--short of calling the law, there is nothing to force him to leave. Unusual though it may be, a volunteer could become unruly, but it is difficult to ask him to leave because he is a volunteer and, as such, has a right to be there.

2) Some reward needs to be provided for volunteers whether it be a free lunch, pizza at the end of the day, or refreshments during the move. As a result, the free help isn't so free after all.

3) It is difficult to determine how many volunteers will be available. It is a good idea for libraries to have preregistration for the volunteers in order to get some idea of the number that will be available. However, if people must travel across town to sign up, many may not be willing to do so. Thus, there may be a number of volunteers show up on moving day who have not pre-registered. Can the library use extra workers or will they just get in each other's way? Who shall turn away the extras and with what excuse? How does one refuse someone who is graciously offering his time and effort? The ill will thereby created may not be good PR for the library.

4) Volunteers may not show up. Even those who have pre-registered may not show up if they find something more interesting to do, have a more urgent obligation or if the weather is anything other than warm and sunny. Those who are ill probably feel no obligation to call in sick. If they do try, whom do they call? It can be very exasperating to plan a move with a certain number of workers only to discover at the last moment that the work force has been drastically reduced.

5) There is a certain element of risk involved in that volunteers are an unknown entity. They may or may not be dependable. They may or may not be good workers and may lack the capacity to follow even the simplest directions.

Libraries moving materials of some value may be better off not turning volunteers loose in their collection. Because a volunteer force is such an unknown entity, a professional or nonprofessional book thief could sneak into the group. Though certainly not exclusively a problem of a volunteer group, even the most honest volunteer might be tempted by seeing a book he finds particularly appealing; he might even consider it his due for the services he has rendered. Libraries in large metropolitan areas may find that volunteers in varying states of sobriety are eager to help in order to get the free lunch that's being provided--a situation which may not be a problem if the library has anticipated it and is prepared to handle it.

6) Volunteers don't understand how the library works. Due to their lack of understanding, getting a stack of books to the new location--regardless of order--might be the only important issue for them. They might not understand the classification system, so if books are dropped, they may be unable to replace them into the correct order.

7) Volunteers don't care if they do it right. If the books are placed on the shelf out of order, or if a drawer of shelflist cards is dropped the cards are replaced in the drawer in random order, that mistake won't be discovered until tomorrow (or later), by which time the volunteer will be long gone. They have no direct continuing relationship to the library and so, may not care how well the job is done, as long as it is done.

If books are dropped in the mud, the volunteer only knows that by tomorrow the mud will dry. He won't be here tomorrow to watch the pages warp and doesn't realize that the stained book may be needed by others frequently during the next twenty-five years it spends on the shelf. He doesn't know that the library just paid twice the list price for the book because it's currently out of print and a valuable addition to the collection.

PAID VOLUNTEERS.

A paid volunteer is a worker who offers his services but is remunerated for them. The recruiting methods for paid volunteers can be similar to those used for unpaid volunteers: The library simply announces that it needs a certain number of workers to help with the move of the library. Interested workers are told to fill out an application or appear for a personal interview, or both. The paid volunteer is distinguished from another type of paid worker in that he is someone who does not normally move libraries for a living nor is he regularly employed by the library; he offers his services to the library on a one-time basis in exchange for salary.

While not eliminating all the problems of using volunteers, using paid volunteers does minimize some of the risks. However, salaries are an expense which the library must be prepared to pay if this method is used.

The basic differences between volunteers and paid volunteers is that the paid volunteers may be screened. Those which do not appear to be satisfactory either from the application form or from the personal interview, need not be hired.

Paid workers may also be dismissed from their duties. Since they are working for a salary, unsatisfactory behavior jeopardizes that salary, resulting in potentially fewer discipline problems. The paid worker, then, may be told what time to show up, what to do while he is there, and what time to quit.

LIBRARY STAFF.

Because the size of the staff is usually proportionate to the size of the library--meaning that libraries of all sizes tend to be understaffed--it is normally impossible to undertake any type of major move using library staff only. It would take a small library with a staff the size of that normally found in a large library to be able to carry out a move without using outside help.

Library staff should be involved in a move as much as possible because they are the people who know the library best. The are the ones who understand its collection, its services, its various functions. It is library staff who will take the care to see that it is done right; if items are misplaced, it is they who will be inconvenienced later. The clerk who just spent three days filing shelflist cards will be especially careful to see that the drawer is not dropped.

When additional help is hired, as is usually the case, library staff can be used as supervisors--each in his or her own area of expertise. Having sufficient personnel to supervise each area will make the work flow more smoothly and help temporary help understand the importance of what they are doing.

Upper management must be cautioned to be fair to their staff during a move. It is not fair to expect the staff to fulfill their normal functions from 9 to 5 and then be full of energy to help with the move all evening. They might be given overtime wages for their moving time or compensatory time off, but there should be some additional compensation to provide them with an incentive and a reward for all their extra effort.

BUILDINGS-AND-GROUNDS STAFF.

Some libraries may have a buildings-and-grounds staff (i.e. maintenance crew). While buildings-and-grounds people have more of an emotional tie to the library than volunteers, they still may lack the understanding of how a library functions. It might be wise to reserve the buildings-and-grounds staff to help with moving the furniture, stacks and other large equipment, while depending on another type of worker to move the collection.

Because buildings-and-grounds staff already belong to the organization and produce no added salary expense, administrators often tend to use them. The move director should bear in mind that moving the library may be just another burden placed on top of their already heavy work load by the administration and should frequently remind them how much their services are appreciated. A sympathetic and enthusiastic buildings-and-grounds team can be a deciding factor in accomplishing a successful move, and the library staff need to show their support and encouragement.

PROFESSIONAL HELP.

Let us state dogmatically that whenever possible, a professional mover should be hired. A professional mover is someone whose primary occupation is to complete the function of moving a library from one location to another. The professional mover possesses the knowledge and expertise, the labor force, and the equipment to accomplish the move in the most efficient and effective manner possible; if he does not do so, he--not the library--must withstand any additional expense.

How the move will be accomplished and what portion of that move is to be done by the professional mover is something that must be spelled out in the contract--and before that if bids are let.

Libraries who wish to have the expertise of a professional without the great expense might try a combination method of contracting the professional to provide the expertise and the equipment while the library provides a staff of paid volunteers to perform the actual labor. In dealing with a professional mover, it is not a recommendable practice to provide a staff of unpaid volunteers because of some of the problems previously mentioned; should such problems occur, the professional may refuse to deal with the volunteers or the move may be delayed to such an extent that the professional mover charges for additional time above and beyond that which was contracted for.

Many of the factors which must be considered in hiring a professional mover are discussed in greater detail in the next chapter.

CHAPTER 16

Hiring a Professional Moving Company.

Some libraries choose to hire a professional moving company to move the library. Basically, there are two types of companies to choose from.

1) General professional movers, such as may be found in the yellow pages of the local telephone directory. Usually dealing with moving homes and household goods, these companies move many different types of items. Some may have experience moving libraries.

In searching for a moving company of this type, establish contact by telephone and inquire if the company has experience moving a library or similar operation. If the answer is affirmative, inquire what libraries they have moved in the local area. Then, contact those libraries for a recommendation.

2) Specialized library movers. There are a number of such companies scattered throughout the country. A partial list has been included in the appendix.

These companies are usually well represented at national professional conventions, such as the American Library Association national convention. Tour the exhibits, and they will be easy to locate. Stop and inquire at their booths. Always ask what libraries they have moved previously and get recommendations (pro or con) from those libraries.

Specialized movers can also be located through the professional literature. Check the classified sections of *Library Journal*, *American Libraries*, or *Wilson Library Bulletin*. As always, get a list of libraries which they have moved in the past and call or write those libraries for a recommendation.

BID PROPOSALS.

After several potential movers have been located and the undesirable ones removed from consideration, if the remaining companies are more or less equal, the next step might be the letting of bids.

It is also possible to publish the announcement of the letting of bids and let any willing companies make an offer. The proposal must be so thorough and accurate as to keep out of the running any company which cannot provide the type of service the library wants.

Before bids can be let, however, the library must already be past the stage of measuring the collection, as outlined in chapters four and five. In order for a mover to bid accurately on the cost of moving the collection, it must be predetermined exactly what the parameters of the move are: the size of the collection; the distance; the dates of the move; exactly what is to be moved, if anything, in addition to the collection; how much labor will be provided by the library and how much by the professional; how much of the preliminary work (such as building ramps, removing doors or windows, etc.) will be done by the library's own buildings-and-grounds crew; and how quickly the move must be accomplished.

If the move is to occupy other than normal working hours, this must also be specified, as professional moving companies may be obligated to pay their workers for overtime if they are expected to work nights or weekends.

It must be spelled out clearly what will happen in the event of unfavorable weather--which, itself, must be defined; how bad is too bad? Professional moving companies may be losing money if the move is delayed, either because they are losing the opportunity for other work on that date or because they may have to pay their workers for showing up, whether the move takes place or not.

If any of the factors in the proposal for bids are changed after a bid has been accepted, the library may face legal action unless bids are reopened to all prospective companies. It is, therefore, imperative, that the proposal be prepared as accurately and carefully as possible. If a factor is omitted, it might be more cost-effective to let a subcontract rather than change the original proposal.

In the bid proposal, specify that the library is open, by appointment, for inspection of the materials that are to be moved, the old location, and the new location. Without an on-site inspection, a mover might not be aware that he will need to construct a ramp from the third floor window for the removal of materials. Or he might not realize that materials must be hauled by hand or booktruck a hundred yards to the nearest driveway.

Appointments to view the collection and the premises should be made with the move director. To avoid giving one mover an unfair advantage over the others, each mover should have an individual appointment.

If individual appointments are not possible, a group tour should be offered simultaneously to all bidders. It is not fair to give a group tour to some companies and an individual tour to others.

CONTRACTS.

Once a bid has been accepted, the next step is to draw up the contract. This should be done, as should the proposal for bids, in consultation with the library's legal advisor. It is important for the legal advisor and the move director to work together closely enough so that the legal advisor understands everything that is involved in the move. Legal advisors are usually not professional librarians, nor are they expected to be. It is up to the move director to help the advisor understand the move from the librarian's viewpoint so that his legal counsel can be accurate and to the point.

Every variable must be spelled out in the contract, just as it must be in the proposal, with the addition of further details that may not have been covered in the proposal. The proposal, for example, may not have specified the technique that will be used for the move, nor the supplies that are necessary. The contract must define the method and spell out the list of supplies and who will provide them.

The contract should specify the date for the move and possible alternate dates. It should clarify on what bases the move may be postponed and who shall make such determination. It should delineate lines of authority, particularly to what extent the employees of the professional moving company shall be governed by the move director. It should specify any penalty that shall be paid by either party in case of postponement or default and the amount of liability to be borne by the moving company in case of damage to the materials.

Any factor which is not clearly spelled out in the contract is a potential problem. Therefore, the writing and negotiation of the contract should be allowed as much time as necessary until both parties are fully satisfied with its terms and stipulations. It is important to allow ample lead time so that negotiations are not rushed by a fast approaching move date.

A sample moving contract is included in appendix A.

CHAPTER 17

Communicating with staff.

Communication is one of the principles of good management. Its effects for good or ill are even more readily apparent than usual in a situation like a move in which every sector of the community is directly affected.

It has long been true that when the official channels of communication are empty, the unofficial channels fill up. When there is no official communication of what's going on, the grapevine will be full; rumors will fly fast and furiously. Misinformation will be rampant. The best way to stop the rumors--before they get started--is to provide plenty of "official" information to those involved.

Because a move is a time of uprooting, or unsettling, it must also be a time of stroking, of back-patting, of consoling. The "little guy" at the bottom of the ladder must be able to see how important his piece is to the whole puzzle and how much we're counting on him to do his part. Some of this must come, naturally, from his direct supervisor, but some of it also must come from top management--particularly in a large organization where those in the lower ranks may easily feel they have been overlooked by those at the top. After all, the "little guy" is being moved from his desk too, and his office is being reassigned--potentially a traumatic experience. We must exercise care to show that we recognize and understand his feelings and empathize with them.

If the "little guy" is expected to complete a task by a certain time and date, he will do it more willingly if he understands the relation of that task to the entire move and why he has been give particular time restraints. What may seem to him as being months too soon, may, in fact, be barely in the nick of time if the move is to proceed smoothly and as planned. His cooperation will be easier to gain if he understands this.

Library staff members in public service areas will constantly be receiving questions about the move from those they serve. Even those in non-public areas will receive questions from families and friends. Needless to say, it creates a poor public image for library personnel to be uninformed about what is going on in regards to the move. If the staff member resents being uninformed, his attitude is bound to show through and cast the library in a poor light. Library staff members need to be informed about the move so that they may give information which is timely and accurate.

It is particularly important that staff members feel part of the process. They need to feel that the new library is theirs, that they belong and are welcome there. If they are feeling uprooted from their old office, they must feel that there is a new office being built specifically for them. Tours of the new building for library staff members are extremely important, with the tours increasing in frequency as the building nears completion.

Good communications with the internal community at all levels is vital to a smooth transition and should have high priority. The first step is to develop a communications hierarchy. Establish a procedure via which news about the move will be communicated. The larger the organization, the more proscribed this hierarchy will have to be. Whatever the size of the library, communication must be frequent and it must be ample. The important thing is that everyone involved receive information which is timely, accurate, and consistent.

NEWSLETTER.

Particularly in larger libraries, a newsletter is a technique that works well for disseminating information. Unfortunately, it is a technique that also requires quite a bit of time--a technique the move director will probably not have time to undertake in addition to his many other duties. Such a task might be relegated to the move director's secretary, depending upon the amount of time that that person is involved in other aspects of the move, or to another staff member whose responsibilities are not too heavy during the move.

The move director serves as editor-in-chief, since he is the person with the latest official information on the move. While not directly involved with the writing, he should retain final editorial approval before the news is released. Naturally, he will be the primary source of much of the news.

The move director must decide what type of news is to be included in the newsletter and to whom it will be distributed. If is "housekeeping" type news with details of what's happening when, such as specifications that members of the cataloging department are to have their personal belongings packed and ready to be moved by a week from Friday, it will probably be considered an in-house document to be given only to those directly affected by the move. It might, on the other hand, be a public relations document to keep the community at large informed of what's going on; in this case, the move might be described in general terms, leaving out specific "housekeeping" details.

A time frame must be established for the intervals at which the newsletter will be published. Probably, it should not be less frequently than once a week, with releases increasing in frequency as the move draws nearer. Close to the time of the move, it might be wise to distribute the newsletter daily, or even twice daily.

BULLETIN BOARD.

Another method of communication with staff which works well in a smaller library is the bulletin board. As there are updates on the move, bulletins are posted at some predetermined place. To assure that everyone gets to see the bulletins without having to check the board constantly, it is well to post the bulletins at an established time. In the early stages, such time might be every Monday morning. As time draws closer to the moving date, the postings must become more frequent, such as every morning at ten o'clock.

The advantage of the newsletter is that everyone receives his own copy which he can keep on file and mark up any way he chooses, highlighting those areas which are of particular personal concern.

The bulletin board method is less expensive simply because of the savings in not making and distributing copies. It is also far less time consuming because copies need not be made and distributed.

STAFF MEETING.

An alternate method of communicating with staff is the staff meeting. Regular meetings are scheduled at which news about the move will be updated. As with the previous two methods, these meetings will need to increase in frequency as the move date draws near.

One of the advantages of the staff meeting is that it is less expensive than either of the other two methods. A very positive factor is that it is the only method which provides a means for feedback, for clearing up any problems or questions the staff may have.

A problem with the staff meeting is that it is usually dependent on the individual staff member to take notes on those items which are of interest to him. Notes may be taken inaccurately or incompletely as the staff member becomes engrossed in the discussion and neglects to write things down.

A good way to ensure accuracy and permit the interchange of ideas is to use the technique of handouts in conjunction with the staff meeting. Vital information is reproduced and distributed to those present. Care should be taken to check attendance so that copies may be distributed to those who are absent.

Another problem with the staff meeting is the amount of time it requires. Simply getting to and from the meeting site may require more time than would normally be spent reading a bulletin or newsletter.

If meetings are held after hours, those involved must work overtime in order to attend the meeting. Overtime pay could impact a budget which is already taxed to the limit with building and moving expenses.

On the other hand, if staff meetings are held during normal working hours, they pull the staff away from their regular jobs at a time when everyone may be especially busy preparing for the move.

If the library is open at the time of the meetings, it is inevitable that some staff members will miss the meeting in order to attend to those patrons using the library.

It is also important to communicate with those in the higher echelons of the organization, those who may not be directly involved in the move. Rarely is the move director (or the library director) on top of the heap; almost always there is a higher authority: the principal, the superintendent, the board of trustees, the dean, or the president. If this person or group of people are to lend us their cooperation or the authority of their office, it is imperative that they understand what we need and expect of them. If, for example, we expect the president to give an executive order to the maintenance staff that all office furniture be moved between October 25 and November 1, he must understand why such an order is important to the move. His understanding it proportional to the amount of information he receives.

Each library must evaluate its particular situation to determine which type of communication will work best.

CHAPTER 18

Communicating with the public

Of equal importance with internal communication is external communication. Libraries have a public to serve. Ultimately, it is to serve *that* public that the move is being undertaken. Nonetheless, it is service to that public which is disrupted during the process of the move. If we are to remain in their good graces, we must communicate with them so they will understand the process and why it is being undertaken.

If, for example, patrons are consistently unable to obtain--or able to obtain only with some delay--the materials they wish to borrow because the materials have now been moved to another location, we need to explain the situation to them before they become frustrated with a library which cannot meet their needs.

There are a number of ways libraries can communicate with patrons, the effectiveness of each method being dependent upon the individual situation. The suggestions that follow are only a few of many.

A NEWSLETTER. Those libraries which regularly publish a newsletter which is circulated to their patrons will find it a natural place to include articles on the progress of the move. Libraries which have no newsletter may wish to begin one just for the duration of the move with the purpose of keeping the public informed. If the expense of circulating a newsletter is too great, even a one page flyer which can be left on the circulation desk for patrons to pick up will be enormously helpful.

A BULLETIN BOARD. A less expensive option than the newsletter is the bulletin board. Displays can be changed regularly (e.g. weekly) or only as events happen which would make updating necessary. Displays might include a written word from the move director or library director, giving the schedule of moving events which are to occur in the next week or two. Or it might include a detailed explanation by a member of the staff on some step of the process which his department has recently undertaken, is currently undertaking, or plans to undertake in the near future. Photographs, maps and diagrams, charts, or even detailed sketches of such items as booktrucks to be used during the move will make interesting display materials and help people feel that they're being informed about the move of their library.

THE MEDIA. The media must not be overlooked as great ways to disseminate information to the public, often at no cost to the library. While, universally, moving a library is not a rare occurrence, it may occur only once in a lifetime in a given location, and seldom more frequently than once every twenty years or so. Because it is a relatively rare occurrence, the media are usually delighted to give the event ample coverage.

Many libraries, though they may not realize it, have, in some form or another, a public relations office. Businesses often have their own advertising departments whose specific function is to write advertising copy and produce press releases. Every advantage should be taken of the talents of these people for writing about the move.

Colleges and universities usually have an office of institutional advancement (disguised under varying titles) which is staffed with someone whose function is to write press releases of university events. The library which develops a good working relationship with this person will often find it is given extensive media coverage with no expense nor effort other than that required to answer a few questions or grant an interview from time to time.

Newspapers have staff members whose regular assignment is to cover school and educational news. School librarians can find out via their administrative offices who is assigned to their district. Often, the school district has someone who serves as liaison to the press and who can relay information about the move to the reporters.

Public libraries might get their *Friends of the Library* group to handle the publicity of the move as a special project.

Television stations are always looking for "filler" and human-interest stories. They will be interested in covering a library move, particularly if the library is being moved in some interesting or unusual way, such as the "bucket brigade" method, using the Boy Scouts as volunteers, or by building a conveyor belt across the main thoroughfare of town. Even though they may not be interested in events leading to the move, rare is the TV station which will reject an invitation to witness and film the proceedings on moving day.

Whatever office is used, or even if the move director must do it himself, a press release should be sent to all the local papers at each phase of the move, and particularly on moving and dedication days. And don't forget press releases for the professional journals.

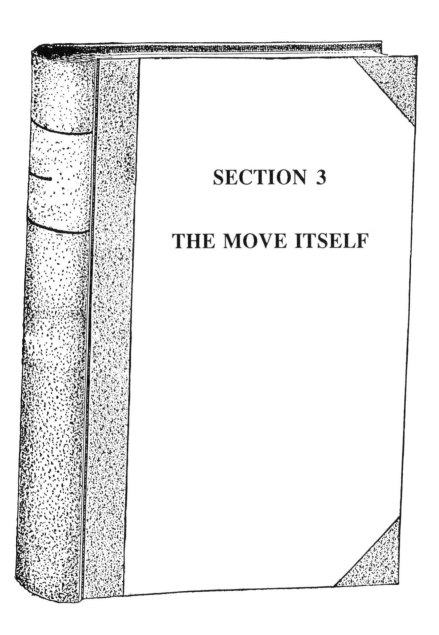

SECTION 3

THE MOVE ITSELF

CHAPTER 19

On moving day

A scenario.

When the goal is to move the books in as brief a time as possible and to have every book in place on the proper shelf at the end of the move, the following is a tried-and-proven method that works well. It may be done with or without professional movers and using volunteers or paid staff.

If the library chooses, a professional mover can be hired to do any necessary construction work--such as ramps--and to provide any needed supplies, and whatever vehicles may be needed, including drivers. The library will supply the actual work force to carry out the move, with the professional providing only guidance and the above mentioned items.

There are several preparatory steps which it is assumed have taken place before the morning of moving day:

1) The collection has been measured, both in number of volumes and linear footage.

2) Based on the measurements, it has been determined exactly in which stack a given book is to be placed in the new location.

3) Stacks in both locations have been clearly marked, with the designations in the old library corresponding directly to the row and stack where those books are to be delivered in the new library.

4) The route has been designated and clearly marked. All bugs have been worked out so that teams moving in opposite directions do not interfere with each other. All provisions for lowering books from the third floor, for example, have been made. Any doors or windows which may block passage have been removed; everything is ready and in place.

5)   The time-and-motion study has been conducted and the results tabulated. It is known how many workers are necessary to move the collection and how long it will take.

6)   Based on the time-and-motion study, workers have been hired. Whether volunteer, paid, or professional, they know when and where to report on moving day, for how long, and what will be expected of them. They have been prepared to face the task at hand and will discover no unpleasant surprises.

7)   All the necessary supplies (e.g. boxes, dollies, tape, etc.) are in place and ready to go.

Begin the day with a staff meeting at which the plan for the day is clearly laid out. Reemphasize who the supervisors are and what their areas of responsibility will be. Each worker should know who his supervisor will be. Each supervisor should know the scope of his responsibility--when to handle the problem himself and when to go to his supervisor.

Make specific team assignments. Let each worker know what his duties will be and what's expected of him.

After the meeting, allow a few minutes for everyone to get to his place and for training. Schedule the move to begin at a certain time, say in forty minutes.

Workers may be assigned to the following areas:

1) **Box makers:** If the library is using cardboard boxes which need to be assembled, for at least the first part of the move, a portion of the crew must be assigned to the task of assembling the boxes and supplying them to the pullers. These workers might later become pullers or another part of the work crew.

2) **Pullers:** Their primary responsibility is to remove the books from the shelves in the old library. The books are placed in the box as they are pulled from the shelf, spine up--though preservationists will argue that they should be placed spine down, the primary factor here is expediency--from left to right in shelf order, normally Dewey or LC shelflist order. Books are not to be laid down on their front or back cover, be placed sideways in the box, nor placed on top of one another. Thus, if a box were picked up, rotated so the open top

were toward the Puller and set on a shelf, the books would look exactly as they did before they were pulled except that the box is now around them.

3) **Markers:** Depending on the workflow, the pullers may also do the marking. Markers are armed with a roll of wide masking tape and a dark colored, preferably black, wide felt-tipped marking pen. As a box is filled, the marker reads the origin from the stack (which is identical to the destination), places the tape on the box, and marks the destination shelf.

Where the tape is to be placed on the box, whether on the top, side, or end, will depend on how the boxes are to be stacked and may vary from library to library. Each box must be labelled in such a way that the labels can be read when the boxes are stacked on top of one another. The first box from stack A-1 should be marked A-1-1, the second box A-1-2 etc. The first box from stack S-29 would be S-29-1 and the sixth box from that section would be marked S-29-6.

When all the books from a given section have been boxed, that particular sequence stops--even if a box contains only two or three books. If it were the last box from stack A-1, it would be marked A-1-7. It is imperative that the person doing the marking circle the number of the last box in the sequence for reasons to be explained later.

Depending on the workflow, the Markers could also assume the responsibility for supplying empty boxes to the pullers.

4) **Mover-outers:** The responsibility of the Mover-outers is to remove filled boxes from the aisles and take them to the point at which they will exit the library. Boxes can be equipped with low dollies or hand trucks which the Mover-outers will bring into the aisles empty and take away full. The mover-outers should strive to keep pace with the work flow. They should try to keep the boxes in a section together; yet, they must move quickly enough that the aisles do not become jammed with filled boxes, hampering the work of the Pullers. The Mover-outers might also supply the empty boxes for the Pullers on their return trip.

5) **Loaders:** The Loaders are responsible for taking the boxes delivered by the Mover-outers and removing them from the library. This job often involves heavy lifting and should be reserved for the biggest and strongest members of the team. It is here that boxes might need to be lifted up to a window so they can be sent down a ramp to an awaiting truck. Or they might need to be set onto a conveyer belt or some other form of transportation. If a ramp or elevator is in use, there will need to be another crew at the bottom of such a device. Such a crew will be responsible for taking the books and loading them onto the truck or other type of conveyance. They will also be responsible for unloading the returning empty boxes from the truck and getting them back up the elevator or ramp.[1]

6) **Drivers:** If using motorized vehicles, a crew of one person per vehicle is often sufficient--simply a driver to deliver the vehicle from point A to point B. When there is considerable distance involved or when the driver must fight heavy traffic, he should be relieved of loading, unloading, or any responsibility other than driving so that he may concentrate all his energies on that very important job. If a professional has been hired as driver, he might, by union mandate, be limited to serve only as driver; such matters should be clarified before moving day arrives.

7) **Unloaders:** The Unloaders will meet the arriving vehicle-- motorized, conveyer system, booktruck, etc.--at its destination and unload the boxes from the vehicle onto the dollies, handtrucks, etc., in use at the new building.

8) **Mover-inners:** The Mover-inners receive the books as they are placed onto the dollies by the Unloaders and deliver them to the correct stack area. It is important that the Mover-inners understand

---

[1]An empty ramp is a much faster way of returning empty boxes than the stairway. Simply place an empty box at the bottom of the ramp and use the next empty box to push it upward. When there are no more empty boxes to be used as "pushers," simply save the remaining empties for the next load.

the coding system used to designate the various stack areas and the best route for getting there. The Mover-inners are also responsible for removing the empty boxes from the aisles of the new library and returning them to the Unloaders so that they may be sent to the old library to be recycled.

9) **Shelvers:** Shelvers are responsible for receiving the full boxes at the proper location in the new library, unpacking the books, and shelving them in their new location. They work with the Mover-inners in seeing that the proper boxes reach the correct location.

It is preferable to wait until all the boxes for a given stack have arrived before beginning to unbox and shelve the books. Remember that the Markers in the old library were to have circled the number of the last box to a stack. The shelvers can determine if the last box has arrived by looking for the circled number. If it is present and there is a complete sequence of numbers from 1 through "X," the circled number, they can begin to shelve, knowing that when those boxes are empty, the stack will be full and they'll be ready to move on someplace else.

Boxes should not be unpacked until the sequence is complete. If boxes one through four have arrived and are shelved before box six arrives, other than an unreliable memory, the Shelver has no way to determine whether box five has been shelved or not. It is not apparent from the classification scheme unless one knows the collection intimately enough to realize that titles are missing-- something even most catalogers or reference librarians would be hard put to determine without a shelflist in hand. If box six is then shelved before box five arrives, upon the later arrival of box five, shelving the books in order will require someone with a better understanding of the classification scheme than that which is to be expected from many volunteers.

If, on the other hand, all books wait in boxes at the proper destination until the sequence is complete, it is simply a matter of placing box one on the shelf before box two, box two before box three, etc.

Using this method with ample advance planning, all the hard work is finished before moving day. The move itself will go like clockwork. If the planning has been correctly done, there will be few, if any, snags. The biggest reward will be that when the movers have gone, the books are on the shelf in the proper sequence and the boxes are disposed of, leaving nothing for the library staff except to continue with their regular jobs in their new library.

CHAPTER 20

Office equipment & furniture.

The move director, in combination with the library director, must decide when to move the center of operations from the old building to the new. The most logical time to make the transition is when the office equipment and furniture have been moved so that staff members have at their disposal the materials they need for the performance of their duties. This may be before, during, or after the moving of the collection. However, for the smoothest transition, it is recommended that it occur as close as possible to the time of the actual move itself.

PERSONAL ITEMS

In general, it is best for each individual employee to be responsible for the contents of his or her own office. A sufficient number of packing boxes should be provided to each employee well in advance of the move. The employee is then responsible for packing the items from his own office. Those items which are property of the library will later be moved at the agreed upon time. It must be established and made known beforehand that the employee will be expected to move, at his own expense, any items in his domain which are not properly ready in time for the movers.

A scheme for marking the boxes must be agreed upon beforehand and the information disseminated to all those involved in the move. The marking should tell whom the materials belong to and the location code of the office to which they are to be delivered. It is up to the library to provide to the staff marking pens of such caliber that the markings may be easily seen and read by the movers.

Personally owned items are to be moved by the individual--not left for the moving crew. The library will provide the boxes, but the individual will pack, move and unpack such items as personally owned books, cosmetics, clocks, pen and pencil sets, and other trinkets. As many of these personal items may be fragile or valuable and require special handling, the owner of the items is responsible for their safety and security. The library's responsibility is to see that offices at both ends of the move are secure from theft and hazard so that the items may be left alone overnight in total confidence.

OFFICE EQUIPMENT AND FURNITURE

Who moves the office equipment and how and when it is moved are matters that will be decided based upon the situation of the individual library.   Those libraries which have their own maintenance staff may choose to have them do the moving of the offices, even though a professional mover may have been hired to move the collection. Using the library's own maintenance staff will cut expense considerably. Also, as the offices may not be moved at the same time as the collection, it will avoid the necessity of hiring the professional for two separate moves--perhaps several days apart.

A determination must be made beforehand as to which pieces of furniture and equipment are to be moved and to where. Whatever will not be moved to the new building should be marked and, if possible, moved out of the way beforehand to allow extra room on moving day.

A helpful device will be a floorplan of the new building with the location of each major piece of furniture marked thereon.   If the drawings are made to scale, pieces of paper furniture can be made and moved about on the drawing for help in developing the scheme for final placement. As always, it is certainly easier to move paper than to move furniture.

Once the detailed floorplan has been developed, each item should be marked on the plan with a code number. A copy of the floorplan of his office should be given to each employee. The individual employee is responsible for marking each item of furniture in his office with the same code as on the floorplan.

If offices will have room numbers, they should be used in the code. If, for example, the director's office is room 211, the code for each item for that office should begin with "211." Individual items may then be assigned a letter code, perhaps even a mnemonic code, for example:

211c	director's chair
211d	director's desk
211f	director's file cabinet.

The items of furniture must be marked in an obvious spot with letters at least one inch high. A felt tip marking pen and a piece of wide masking tape are ideal for the job. Consistent placement of the marks in a pre-determined location will facilitate the job of the movers on moving day.

Then, a master plan should be given to the person who will be responsible for moving the furniture.

COMPUTER EQUIPMENT

Computer equipment must be handled carefully, both because of its fragility and its value. In most cases, it will be preferable for the library staff, or at least the library's own maintenance staff to oversee the moving of such equipment.

The moving of the equipment must be coordinated with the moving of the furniture on which it is to be placed. It is of little value, for example, to exercise great care in moving an expensive printer only to place it on the floor of the new facility, later to be tripped over by a mover with his arms full of boxes.

It is highly recommended that the person in the library with the greatest expertise in computer equipment and software be assigned the task of overseeing the move of all such items. This person should be given decision-making authority as to how and when the items will be moved. It is his decision how items will be packed and who will move them. It is his responsibility to disseminate information to all those responsible for packing and moving the items.

Equally sensitive is the software which is used by the library. Because software is a magnetic medium, great care must be exercised to see that it is not exposed to any type of magnetic field during the move.

Floppy disks have several particular concerns: They must not be packed in such a manner that would allow them to be bent or crushed in any way. They should also be protected from extremes of temperatures. Manufacturers' recommendations are that they be kept between 50 and 125 degrees Fahrenheit (10 to 52 degrees centigrade). A move during the summer or winter months might easily exceed those extremes. Be especially mindful during the summer that, while the outside temperature may only be in the seventies or eighties, it can reach extreme levels inside an enclosed metal vehicle. A good rule of thumb to follow is that if a person or a pet would be uncomfortable, so would floppy disks.

Floppy disks are very sensitive to dust, dirt, and fingerprints. They should be transported only by someone who has experience in handling them and *who is aware that there are floppy disks included in the shipment.* It is a seemingly trivial detail, but it is extremely important that the person responsible for moving office equipment be made aware that he is carrying floppies and that they require special treatment.

As many floppies are owned by, or at least assigned to, specific individuals, it is recommended that each person be made responsible for transporting the floppies in his care, just as he is for his personal items. Even so, employees must be reminded to exercise great care in packing their floppies. To put them in the same box with a lidless jar of instant tea or a bottle of perfume could spell disaster to the tune of several years' worth of work.

OCLC TERMINALS

Many libraries will be faced with the problem of moving OCLC terminals. It must be emphasized that it is not permissible under the terms of the OCLC contract simply to disconnect a terminal, move it, and reconnect it in the new location. While the procedure is much simpler for a dial-up terminal than for one which is hardwired via a dedicated line, there is still a specific protocol which must be followed. Each OCLC subscriber with an M300 workstation should have received from OCLC upon receipt of the terminal a ten-page handout called the "User's Guide to M300 Workstation Installation." If the library staff cannot locate this publication, they should contact their network or OCLC for a copy of publication 8508/2917-2M, OCLC. This booklet outlines the necessary steps for installing the M300 workstation, whether it be the original installation or a reinstallation. According to this document, it is the user's responsibility before a service agent arrives to perform the installation to:

1. Provide proper electrical outlets and an appropriate work area and work surface. Required are

   > Four, 3-prong, 60 Hz, 120-VAC outlets, capable of delivering 450 watts and as a group connected to one 15-amp circuit breaker for installation of the M300 system unit, modem, station termination, and test equipment or printer.

   > At least two outlets of the same type for each additional Workstation.

2. If the Workstation will be used as a dial-up terminal with the OCLC Online System, provide and install a dial-access modem and telephone connection.[1]

The following information is direct from OCLC:

---

[1]*User's Guide to M300 Workstation Installation* Dublin, Ohio: Online Computer Library Center, August 1985.

...If the institution moving the equipment is a member of a Network they should receive all necessary information from their Network. If the institution is not a member of any Network (one we refer to as an "Independent Institution") they would follow the same procedure, but they will be contacting OCLC directly.[2]

The Independent Institution should contact the Installation Services Coordinator of the Network Administration Section.... Once this contact is made, OCLC will send the appropriate request forms accompanied by all necessary information and guidelines. The personnel of Installation Services [have organized] a detailed manual that describes the step-by-step process of completing a "Terminal Move Request"....

...Concerning the different procedures of moving terminal(s) with dial-access connection versus terminals with a dedicated line, OCLC must be notified in the case of any terminal move. If a dedicated line is involved, naturally the phone company must also be involved to a great extent. This is coordinated through OCLC. If the Independent Institution wishes to move terminal(s) with a dial-access connection they may coordinate the move themselves. OCLC should then be notified of the new location of the terminal(s) so that the records at OCLC be accurate. In the case of an OCLC supplied dial-access terminal being moved, the Independent Institution should know if they will be changing regions of OCLC's Maintenance Coordinators.

Once OCLC receives the Terminal Move Request OCLC calculates two different time-lines. If the terminal

---

[2]Installation Services Coordinator, Network Administration Section, OCLC, Online Computer Library Center, 6565 Frantz Road, Dublin, Ohio 43017-0702. Phone: (614) 764-6000 TWX 810-339-2026.

is to be moved to another location within the same premise, thirty-three working days should be allowed once the request is entered into the OCLC system. If the terminal is to be moved to a location off premise, fifty-five working days should be allowed to complete the request.

Since...information can be outdated rather quickly, the accurate cost of completing such a move should be obtained at the time the institution decides to move their equipment.[3]

Members of other bibliographic utilities should contact their network representative or the utility to inquire as to the requirements of their particular utility. Contact should be established several months in advance of the projected moving date.

BOOKSTACKS

It must be borne in mind at all times that books can be moved no faster than the shelving for them is made available. The disassembling, moving, and reassembling of the shelving, therefore, can be the weak link in the chain, the road hog who will slow down all the traffic behind him.

The library that does not need to move its old book shelving to its new location is as fortunate as it is rare.

On the other end of the continuum is that library which will acquire no new shelving but only move the current shelving to the new location. This can be the single, most complicated factor of the entire moving process, as the shelving cannot be moved until it is emptied and the books removed from that shelving cannot be shelved until the shelving is reassembled in the new location. The problem thus created by this double jeopardy is one of intermediate

---

[3]Martindale, Lowell A., OCLC Product Administration Assistant. Letter to author.

storage; the books must be moved somewhere so the shelving can be moved, but they cannot be housed in the new location because shelving is still nonexistent.

What is to be done with the books for intermediate storage will depend upon the size and distance of the move and the situation of the individual library. If there are enough booktrucks available, a simple solution is simply to move the collection (perhaps a portion at a time) to booktrucks and leave it there until the shelving is reassembled in the new location. The booktrucks may then be used to move the books to the new location where they will be shelved directly from the trucks.

Another possible solution involves the use of cartons or boxes. Enough of the collection is removed from the shelves and boxed to allow a given section of shelving to be disassembled and moved--the boxes being clearly labelled as to their new location. Then, the books are transported in the boxes to the new location.

Depending on how cramped the old and new quarters are, there might be a problems in finding sufficient space to store the books which have been boxed or placed on trucks without violating space that is needed for the work crews to get their job done. If vehicles are used to transport the books between locations, it might be possible to use the vehicles themselves as temporary storage. Naturally, if those vehicles belong to a professional mover or are rented on a time contract, such an option could raise the cost of the move considerably. Nevertheless, it might be cheap when compared with the alternatives.

The most common scenario is that library which will order some new shelving for the new library and move all or most of its current shelving to the new location. Problems can be kept to a minimum with careful planning.

A good rule to keep in mind is that, insofar as possible, the shelving to be removed should be the first to be emptied and the last to be filled. If moving in call-number order, for example, use the new shelving for the first items to be moved--the Dewey 000s or the LC "A"s. Thus, those portions of the collection can be removed from the old shelves and placed on the new which are already assembled. When the old sections are emptied, they can be disassembled and moved. If the old shelves are used for the end of the call number sequence--the 900s or the "Z"s--the maintenance crew has sufficient lead time to get them disassembled, moved, and reassembled before they are needed.

Because the collection is being more widely spaced in the new location with entire shelves and portions of shelves left empty for expansion, new shelves are going to be "gobbled up" more quickly than old shelves become available. If the general rule of expansion[4] is followed, the new shelving will be occupied at approximately twice the rate at which the old shelving becomes available.

This will result in an effect of decreasing returns, with a mathematical factor of one half. Let's look at the example of a small library: The ABC Library will have two hundred stacks in its new location. Of these, 100 are newly purchased stacks and 100 are being moved from the old location. On moving day, the 100 new stacks are assembled and ready to receive books. Because stacks are being filled twice as quickly as they are being emptied, by the time all 100 stacks are full, 50 stacks in the old location will have been emptied. If the 50 stacks are then disassembled, moved, reassembled and filled, there will be 25 empty stacks in the old location. When the 25 stacks are moved and filled, there will be 12 and a half stacks empty in the old location, etc. It is to be expected, therefore, and must be allowed for in the time-line that eventually the book movers will catch up with the maintenance crew which is moving the stacks and will have to wait for them to assemble more stacks before more books can be shelved.

In view of the above situation, it is helpful to have a sizeable portion of the collection in transit at any given moment, and, of course, to have the book shelvers working at a pace behind that of the maintenance crew. Again, depending on the situation of the individual library, it may be wise to have book shelvers start several hours, or a day or two AFTER those who are removing the collection from the old shelves. Then, the last of the books can be unshelved and in transit by the time the book shelvers get ready to

---

[4]Top and bottom shelves and one third of each occupied shelf is left empty for later growth.

begin shelving that section, allowing the maintenance workers ample lead time to move and assemble the shelving.

How well the delaying tactic works will depend on the method being used for the move. If the "bucket brigade" or the "walking in line" method is used, the delaying tactic may not be possible at all, as the books are going to travel from their source to their destination much faster than it is humanly possible to disassemble, move, and reassemble shelving.

Another possible solution is to schedule the move on two nonconsecutive days. Thus, the maintenance crew has a day in between during which they can carry out their activities with considerably less pressure.

It must be stressed that the pressure on the maintenance crew should never reach a level that causes them to become careless in their task; shelving which is not assembled correctly is potentially dangerous. There are documented cases in the professional library literature of deaths and serious injuries attributable to defective or improperly assembled shelving. Proper assembly is particularly important in a situation of loading and unloading wherein an entire range of shelves may be loaded or unloaded on one side, causing additional instability.

Another factor that needs to be considered is the transport of the shelving. Huge, bulky shelving cannot be conveniently moved in and out via the same doors through which there is a constant flow of people bearing books. Either an alternate route must be found, or a break in the flow of books must be scheduled; certainly, the alternate route is the more desirable of the two options but may not always be possible. Can the stacks be moved in and out during a break or during the lunch hour when the book movers are not present? Or perhaps at night?

To what extent must the shelves be disassembled before moving? Certainly the larger the pieces that can be moved, the quicker and easier the move will be for everyone. Could assembled or partially assembled stacks be moved if there were a heavy-duty dolly available? How does the cost of such a dolly compare with the cost of the time and effort that would be expended to completely disassemble and reassemble the stacks?

The King Library of Miami University was faced with the problem of replacing the carpeting in the stacks. When the decision was made that the carpeting should be placed under the shelving rather than cut out and placed around it, those involved in the process decided there had to be an easier way to get the job done than completely disassembling each stack. Using a rolling trailer jack--the same kind used by recreational vehicles--the maintenance crew was able to construct a heavy duty dolly which would move a range of unloaded stacks intact.[5]

It is particularly important that the move director and the person in charge of moving the shelving be in close communication before move day and, together, arrive at some determination of the pace at which the shelving can be moved. The speed with which the move may be made hinges on the rate of shelving more than on any other single issue.

THE CARD CATALOG AND OTHER FILING CABINETS

Variations on the technique used for moving books may be used for the transfer of the card catalog, shelflist, filing cabinets, microfilm and microfiche cabinets, desks, and any other piece of furniture with drawers.

Basically, the drawer itself serves as the transfer vehicle for its contents. If something is already packed neatly in a drawer, why bother to unpack it, box it, move it, unbox it and put it away when it can be moved just as it is?

The first step in the process is to assign a code to the piece of furniture itself. Letter codes, perhaps mnemonic, will serve well, as will be observed in a moment.

Let us look, for example, at the card catalog, which probably has a greater number of drawers than any other single piece of furniture. Because of the sheer weight of the piece, the drawers--but not the

[5]Alley, Brian. "Moving Steel Stacks With a Special Dolly" *Library Acquisitions: Practice and Theory* 6 (1982):253-257.

contents of the drawers--must be removed and shipped separately from the cabinet itself. The problem then becomes one of getting the drawer back into the proper cabinet in the proper order quickly and efficiently.

Each drawer is assigned a sequential consecutive number, starting with number one. If the code for the card catalog is "CC," the code for the first drawer would be "CC-1." The code for the fortieth drawer would be "CC-40," etc. Larger libraries have an advantage in that the drawers of their card catalog are often already numbered.

The complete code for each drawer must be placed on the front of the drawer. We suggest a piece of masking tape in the upper left-hand corner labelled with a marking pen. To the left of this label on the partition between the drawers--on the cabinet front itself, not the drawer front--place another piece of tape with the identical number. When replacing the drawers, the two labels will be right next to each other and, thus, it will be easy to match the two numbers for proper placement.

Depending upon the number of items to be moved and how they are to be moved, it might also be desirable to preface the code number for the individual piece of furniture with a code for the office or room to which it is to be delivered. For example, if there are several card catalogs, the one which is to be delivered to the main reading room might be coded "MR-CC" and its drawers labelled "MR-CC-1," etc.

SPECIAL EQUIPMENT

If the library has equipment which is not its own but rental or loaner equipment or equipment which is under maintenance contract, check with the owner or contract holder before attempting to move it. Some equipment, such as photocopiers, is very sensitive and the owners may prefer to move it themselves. In addition, if the library attempts to move the equipment, it may be held liable for any damages actually or allegedly resulting from the move; a service agreement may be voided.

Before moving such equipment, for economic reasons if for nothing else, the library should try to get the owner/contractor to move it. If he won't move it, it is advisable to acquire a signed permission form releasing the library of any liability for resulting damage, unless, of course, caused by negligence on the part of the library. It is preferable for the library to draw up the form and send it to the other party for ratification so that it is worded properly. Specify that it is to be returned by a certain date well in advance of the move date.

Even if the owner/contractor is not doing the moving, be sure to check with him to see if the equipment requires any special preparation before being moved. Copiers, for example, often need to have the toner, dispersant, and paper trays removed. Some equipment, such as phonographic turntables or cassette decks, have set screws which should be tightened in order to prevent damage. Some types of equipment may require the insertion of insulators or other special preparation to prevent potential damage during a move. Always read the manual and, whenever possible, check with the supplier.

As a rule of thumb, the more sensitive the equipment is, the better it is to let someone else move it and thus assume the responsibility for its safety.

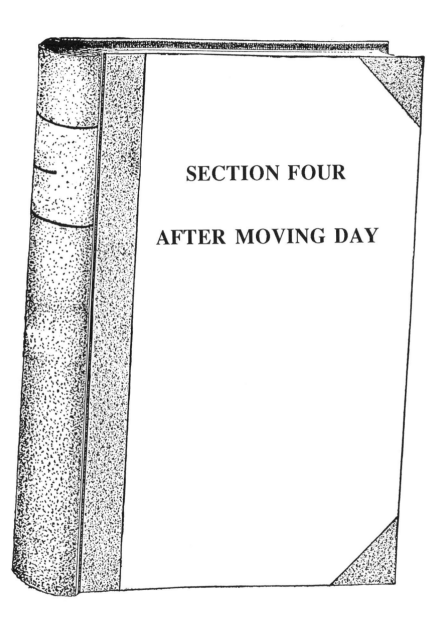

SECTION FOUR

AFTER MOVING DAY

CHAPTER 21

Reading the stacks.

Once the move is finished, there comes the time of finding and tying up the loose ends. It is only with the passage of time that one may determine whether the particular location in which things have been placed is functional or whether it would be desirable to make some adjustment. If the move has been well thought out and planned in advance, such adjustments should be minor, but some moves are inevitable. These adjustments should be expected and budgeted for.

Such adjustments might include things like moving furniture. Perhaps moving the clerk's desk three feet to the left will allow him to see when patrons are queuing up at the circulation counter. Perhaps a cord which is four feet longer will allow the phone to be placed in a location which is much more convenient.

One of the largest adjustment may be the shifting of the book collection itself. If the move has been carefully planned on paper, it is totally possible that no shifting will be necessary. Indeed, most moves should occur in this way.

The move technique itself may make additional shifting necessary. If the move has been accomplished using volunteers, especially if they have not been thoroughly trained in moving technique and had that technique drilled into them so they carry out their task as efficiently as robots, shifting may be necessary. Every time a worker loses his place in line, every time a book is dropped, books will end up in the wrong final destination. In a careful move, such mislocation may keep books within a few inches of where they are supposed to be; nevertheless, if the books are to end up in strict call number order, some shifting will be necessary.

By performing an inventory after a move, two tasks can be accomplished at the same time and with no additional expense.

Most libraries perform some type of inventory periodically. By scheduling such inventory after the move, it can also serve to place the books in their proper order on the shelves.

Those libraries which do not perform inventory regularly will find it a good idea to do so after a move so that they can be sure the books are--at least once--in the proper order.

One library, which was installing a book theft detection system in its new facility, chose to combine three activities into one after the move: reading the stacks, taking inventory, and preparing each book in the collection for detection by the theft protection system. By combining the tasks, the three jobs were accomplished in one pass through the collection. Many of those books reported missing on the first pass turned up later as they were found misshelved elsewhere.

Patrons (and staff), who for many years may have tolerated misshelved and unlocatable materials because of the cramped quarters in the old building, expect things to be in perfect order in the new facility. While the task is not quite one hundred percent possible, it should be the goal, and there must be adequate provision in the budget for striving toward that goal.

Because the rush and pressing deadlines of the move no longer exist, the regular library staff--presumably composed of experienced and accurate shelvers--can rearrange the books and place them in order at their convenience. In fact, some libraries feel that it is sufficient to accomplish on move day only the moving of the books from one building to the other, without worrying about specific locations. (Careful planning can still streamline the task, however, eliminating a lot of unnecessary extra shifting later.) These libraries plan to have their regular staff shift the entire collection after the move.

There are some conditions under which it will be necessary or even desirable to plan to shift the entire collection after the move, such as those cases in which a section of the new building is not yet ready to receive books on moving day, or when other collections are to be merged into the same call number sequence.

In circumstances in which the collection will be shifted later, it is desirable to designate an area of the new building as temporary shelving. This shelving can then be packed on move day to 100%

of capacity; no room need be left for expansion because the collection will be shifted with room left for expansion before the collection has a chance to grow.

Reading and inventorying the stacks after the move is as necessary to the total process as weeding is at the beginning.

CHAPTER 22

Reward time

As surprising as it may seem, when the move is over, those who have been heavily involved in many months of intensive planning can experience a feeling of let-down, deflation, even depression. The move ends so suddenly that it seems almost anti-climactic. All the stress, the pressure, the worry that has been building for so many months is suddenly and decidedly over. There may come an overwhelming feeling of "what do I do now?"

To avoid these symptoms and the psychological stress they can produce, a special time should be planned for after the move. It is a wise practice not to plan the dedication of the new facility until the move is over, as any type of delay in the move could force a postponement. Therefore, some type of celebration should be planned for those who have been wrapped up in the move. In many cases the official dedication of the facility won't take place for several months.

Such a celebration may or may not involve those workers who have been hired temporarily to help only during the move, but it should definitely include permanent staff who are directly affected.

Often there have been dozens or hundreds of volunteers helping during the move. It would be expensive to reward them all, but perhaps there could be a pizza party at the end of the day after the move. Or they could receive free tickets to some library event. Local businesses might be willing to donate some sort of prize for those who have helped move the library.

Some libraries choose to have a celebration on the evening after the move with some type of special performance being provided free of charge to all those who helped. The performance might be a movie or a concert, but it should be something which will be of interest to the majority.

Any entertainment which is physically or mentally taxing should be avoided. This is a time for celebration, rest, and relaxation. Any type of festivity which is planned should meet those criteria.

Nor should the entertainment be lengthy. If it has been a long moving day, most people are probably physically exhausted and would like nothing better than to get home to bed. This is simply a time to "let your hair down" together and give each other a pat on the back.

A celebration involving just the permanent library staff might be better postponed for a few days until all the loose ends have been tied up and everyone has lost the feeling of disorientation which often succeeds a move. Perhaps planning an activity for the Saturday following the move would be appropriate--a picnic or a potluck supper. The best time is after everyone has had a chance to rest for a day or two, relax and get cleaned up. Few people will enjoy attending a social activity in sweaty, dirty clothes at the end of a long tiring day.

At these festivities is an ideal time to reward those who helped in some special way. If a professional mover was hired, the library might wish to present him a plaque or a certificate in appreciation of his help. Even though he is being paid--and probably quite well-- for his services, what is gained in good will by such a gesture is beyond price.

The library staff has suffered with the move for many months. Some have adeptly carried out their daily routines with movers knocking the plaster dust down around their ears. Such workers need to be told that they are appreciated and that someone is aware of the sacrifices they have made. Even if they grumbled and complained incessantly, such a reward might cause them to perform better in the future--either from gratitude or a guilty conscience.

When the buildings-and-grounds crew of the institution has been involved in the move, they must not be overlooked when it is time to say "thank you." Buildings-and-grounds crews are often "put upon" by the senior administration to perform a task for which they are ill-trained and understaffed. Often, they are asked to work overtime in moving the library after having performed a full day of their regular duties. They are already overworked and underpaid, and asking them to move the library just might be the proverbial straw that broke the camel's back. Receiving some appreciation from the library staff for their services can go a long way in soothing the pain they have suffered.

The move director should receive a special reward. This reward needs to come both from above and from below. Receiving a plaque from the president of the university is nice, but it pales if none of the staff members with whom the move director must work shoulder to shoulder daily bothers to breathe a word of thanks.

On the other hand, demonstrations of appreciation from co-workers are well received, but after months and months of working above and beyond the call of duty--and moving a library is certainly above and beyond the call of duty--the move director needs to hear from his superiors that he has done a superb job in moving 150,000 volumes in three days with no major snags. A certificate of appreciation or a plaque for his office wall is not to much to give. If there is a dedicatory plaque to be installed in the lobby or in the cornerstone, it could be mentioned that "This building was occupied on June 24, 1995, under the direction of move director George Wyckoff."

A financial reward might also be in order for the move director, who has probably put in many hours of overtime on the project and for which he is not recompensed if he is on straight salary. Particularly if the move director has administered his finances wisely, some of what has been saved by his hiring volunteers, or by his acquiring a gift of 1000 beer cartons from the local brewery, or by not having to hire a professional, might be given to him as a bonus in honor of services rendered.

If the situation is such that a financial reward is not possible, the move director might at least receive some compensatory time off. Even a three-day weekend will give the director some positive feelings.

No matter how tight the budget or how regimented the situation, there must be some reward for the move director. Even a house plant, a paperweight for his desk, or an invitation to lunch are ways of saying, "We thank you. We appreciate the good job you are doing." It is extremely important to the emotional well-being of the move director that such a gesture be made.

Finally, everyone who has been heavily involved in the move needs to reward himself proportionately according to his involvement. If the move director has some days off coming to him, he might save them up and take them after the move--he might *have* to save them due to his busy-ness preceding the move. If the staff plans to go out to lunch to celebrate a birthday, why not postpone it for a week and turn it into a celebration of the successful move also? If the director has that book he has been dying to read but has not had time for prior to the move, why not let him lock himself into the office for the afternoon, take the phone off the hook, lie down on the couch he never gets to sit on otherwise, and read? Perhaps just a stroll through the new library wistfully gazing at the books in their new resting places is sufficient reward, but each person needs to plan some reward to himself and save it for that special time--after the move. Unfortunately, in many cases, it may be all the reward he receives.

CHAPTER 23

Dedication of the new facility.

After a library completes the move into a new building, there is usually a ceremony for the dedication of the new facility. As well as a time to celebrate the new facility and all that it implies, this is a time to remember and celebrate all the hard work that was necessary to reach this point.

A dedication ceremony can be as formal or informal as the library chooses to make it, but as occasions for such a celebration in a library are few and far between, we should make the most of it. Pull out all the stops and make the celebration as big, as grandiose, as possible. Remember that the dedication is a reward, a capstone to all that has gone before and a promise of the future. It must not be underdone. As surely as lavishing more attention on the occasion than it deserves will draw the criticism that there was too much hoopla, not doing enough will leave people disappointed, feeling lukewarm. Put forth as much pomp-and-circumstance as the occasion warrants. While a library may choose to celebrate economically, it is extremely important to avoid any impression of parsimoniousness or cutting of corners. An impression of pettiness can go a long way in harming a library's reputation. Elegance need not mean expense.

A dedication ceremony is an opportunity to attract people who are not part of the library community. Examine the pool of potential library patrons and invite as many of them as possible. Invite the general public; do as much publicity as possible and try to reach a segment of the population which is normally untouched by the library.

Invite everyone who is "anyone." Invite local and county officials, state representatives, and even national figures. Invite anyone who might be even remotely connected with or interested in the library.

Here is a partial list of people who might be invited to the dedication:

> The architect who designed the building.
> construction workers, carpenters, etc.
> Those who provided special services:
    plumbing
    elevator
    electrical installation
    air conditioning
    carpeting
    window glass
    woodworking
    doorlocks
> Those who are major suppliers of library furnishings:
    furniture
    shelving
    draperies
    computer equipment
    office equipment
    office furniture
    audio visual equipment
> mayor
> governor
> city council
> county council
> local school board
> law enforcement officials
> nearby librarians
> academic officers of nearby colleges and universities
> local government representatives
> U.S. Senators and Representatives from the district
> staff of the local or state library network
> state librarian and his/her staff
> officers of the state and regional library associations
> ALA officers

> local television stations
> local radio stations
> local newspaper editor
> *Friends of the Library* officers and members
> State or regional *Friends of the Library* organizations
> any groups which regularly hold their meetings at the library
> library donors
> library volunteers
> professional movers
> hired or volunteer movers
> local authors
> student body if an academic library
> leaders of student government if an academic library

Many of those mentioned might not attend the dedication ceremony, but a personal invitation at least sends the message that the library exists and that it cares about the invitee enough to think that his or her presence is important. Libraries which have the budget to do so should send formal, engraved invitations.

There must be a breathing time between the move of the library and the dedication ceremony. Obviously, a breathing time allows those who were heavily involved in the move to rest and recuperate from the physical and emotional strain they have been under.

This period of time allows the staff to get used to performing their duties in the new location. It is a time to iron out any wrinkles in the system. If borrowers' cards are now filed in a different order or in a different location from where they were filed in the old library, workers need time to get used to filing them in the proper place. If the periodicals collection is now down two levels instead of up one, it will take some time to learn to give directions quickly and accurately. Because on dedication day visitors will have lots of questions for them, staff members must be given time to learn the proper answers.

This breathing time allows the library staff time to make sure that things are in perfect order on the day of the ceremony. Any flaws or mistakes which are discovered after occupancy have time to be corrected before being put on public display. Books that may have ended up on the floor because there was no shelving left can be shelved or, at least, hidden away in storage before the public comes in for viewing. The snag in the carpet left by the jagged wheels of the four-hundredth dolly can be fixed. The screws that fell out of the bottom of the chair can be replaced before the mayor sits on it. This may be the library's only day of glory until the next construction project, so make sure everything is its polished best.

The delay between the move and the dedication ceremony also allows adequate time for planning the ceremony. It is a reasonably safe bet that if the staff has to concentrate on the move simultaneously with planning the dedication ceremony, neither one will be done well. Allow sufficient time between the two events for planning and preparations for the ceremony and build in extra time for unforeseen delays.

On the other hand, the ceremony should not be delayed so long that the shiny, new building already begins to show signs of wear: dirt spots on the carpet, graffiti on furniture and walls, scuffmarks from feet placed on those wonderfully low window sills.

Planning something as grandiose as a dedication ceremony is best done by a group. This is one case in which a committee is better. It takes several people with divergent ideas to put together a program which will best represent the library and its community.

The committee should be composed of a diverse group: Library professionals and paraprofessionals, *Friends of the Library* members, trustees, and perhaps a patron or two. An academic library should include faculty members, administrators and student representatives.

The first few sessions should simply be "brainstorming" sessions. Appoint someone as secretary and open the floor for suggestions. Everyone who has any idea at all--no matter how strange, absurd, remote, or expensive--must feel free to speak up. The secretary should record each idea and the name of the person who suggested it. Ideas will spark more ideas. Even those ideas which are absurd may spark some positively brilliant alternatives. Those which are wildly expensive may provoke some reasonable substitute. Do not discount or overrule any idea at the brainstorming sessions. There will be plenty of time later for paring down the list.

After a sufficient number of brainstorming sessions to develop a pool of ideas, it is time to begin narrowing down the list. Begin by throwing out those which are infeasible for one reason or another, but not without first discussing the merits of each and seeing if some adaptation or part of it might be usable. Continue to narrow the list until only the best ideas are left.

When only the best ideas remain, choose enough for a ceremony of reasonable length. Even some of the top ideas may have to be discarded to keep the ceremony within the bounds of human endurance. Many otherwise impressive and inspirational ceremonies have been ruined because the planners--or the speaker--forgot that "the mind can absorb only so much as the posterior can withstand."[1]

When it has been determined which ideas are to be carried out as part of the festivities, responsibilities can be assigned to different members of the committee. One member, for example, might be responsible for inviting the governor to be the dedication speaker and contacting alternates if he declines. Another might be responsible for the physical arrangements of the locale--tables and chairs, a public address system, etc. A third committee member might be responsible for planning whatever food is to be served.

Publicity might be the responsibility of another member of the planning committee. The event should be as widely publicized as possible. Spare no effort in contacting the local media: television, radio, and newspapers. In a small town, the dedication of a new library facility could be a major feature story. Even a large city newspaper might develop it into a major event if there is a writer or editor who is sympathetic toward the library.

Some radio and television stations have talk shows on which guests are interviewed regarding items of concern to the community. A library would do well to secure a spot on such a show. If the library director or a member of the planning committee does not feel at ease being interviewed on the air, perhaps someone else, such as the president of the *Friends of the Library* group would do an excellent job.

---

[1] C. Edward Carroll. School of Library and Information Science, University of Missouri, Columbia, Missouri.

The local media might feel that a library dedication is not worthy of news coverage, but if a well-known personality is to be the dedication speaker, they might feel differently. Let them know who is going to be in attendance and what roles those individuals will play in the program.[2]

The dedication ceremony is a good time for focusing on the three aspects of the library: the past, the present, and the future.

Dedication time is a good time for reminiscing. When, why, and how was the library begun? By whom? What was its original location? How many other buildings has it been housed in? How many volumes were in the original collection? While accuracy is important, those who want a mere listing of facts can find it elsewhere--probably in the library's reference collection; give anecdotes, special problems, hurdles that were overcome, colorful people who were involved in the process. Find a speaker who can bring the history to life.

Next, try focusing on the present: Why was the present construction necessary now? How was the move accomplished? What will the new location mean to the community? How will it affect the services that are offered? What will be available now that was not available before this move?

Naturally, the sequence then progresses to the future: How many volumes can this library hold at capacity? How long will it take to reach that point? What new services might be introduced in the future? Where is library technology going and how will it affect this library?

Entertainment and food are two drawing cards at any ceremony. People who might not otherwise come to a dedication ceremony for

---

[2]The dedication of the library at Bethel College in Mishawaka, Indiana, was covered by local representatives of all three national television networks because the governor was one of the speakers. After the dedication, the reporters bombarded him with questions on several current political issues. On the news that evening, the dedication was featured briefly, but the governor appeared on two or three additional spots discussingthe issues. The fringe benefit was that the exterior of the new library showed up very well in the background.

a library might be enticed into attending if the entertainment appeals to them. Once they have been to the library for the first time, it's much easier to get them to return and, thus, the library will have snagged a new patron.

Search for some kind of entertainment which will have wide local appeal. This might be a puppet show or story hour for the children. Or it might be a "How-to" session for adults. A popular local music group will undoubtedly attract teens. A famous author may attract a diverse group. The dedication can be a useful device in reaching the otherwise unreached elements of the community.

Any time there is an offer of free food or drink, there are also going to be those who abuse the privilege. The individual library must determine what kind of spread it can afford and what type of control, if any, will have to be exercised.

Libraries which are normally very strict about food and drink in the building are often lax during dedication. Remember that vermin find the food equally attractive no matter how or when it gets there. If food is allowed in the library during the dedication, it will be hard to explain to a patron next week why he can't eat a candy bar while he studies. It is best if one area, preferably outside the library building, is designated as the food and drink area and all refreshments are restricted to that area.

A dedication ceremony is a time for thankfulness and for honoring those who have helped make the library what it is today. Each person who has made a contribution no matter how small, be it time, money, expertise, etc., should be recognized in some way. This does not imply that all 547 names of those who have donated five dollars must be read, but they might be listed in the program and publicly thanked en masse during the ceremony. While donors of large sums are often given the most attention, care must be taken to show that each donor is important, no matter how small or large the gift.

Libraries affiliated with religious institutions will want to take time to stop and thank God for their new library. It is right and fitting that they do so.

A natural part of the dedication ceremony is a ribbon-cutting. When there is more than one person who should be afforded the honor of cutting the ribbon, there are several possible solutions.

One is to give each person a pair of scissors and have them cut simultaneously. Another is to use several ribbons, with each honored guest cutting one.

Provide better photos of the library for the media by passing along this tip to those who are cutting the ribbon: When cutting the ribbon to open the library that bears his name, former two-time governor of Indiana and current Secretary of Health and Human Services, Dr. Otis R. Bowen, said, "If there's one thing I've learned from all my years in public office,..." Then, he quickly ducked under the ribbon and turned to face the audience. "...it's never to turn my back to the cameras," he concluded as he snipped the ribbon.

Certainly, the library must offer tours of the new facility. The individual situation will dictate whether these should be self-conducted tours or group tours conducted by a member of the library staff. Visitors must have an opportunity to see the new facility, which, after all, is the whole reason for the gathering. If the library has been offering service for a while, even those who have frequented the new building might like a tour as, normally, they may come in concentrating on the task at hand and not pay much attention to the new surroundings.

Conclude any dedication ceremony with an invitation to all those present to continue using (or to begin to use) their new library. If people go away feeling good about the dedication, they're likely to become library users (and maybe supporters).

MOVING CONTRACT

_____ Library hereby contracts with _____ Storage and Transfer, Inc. to furnish necessary equipment and to coordinate and supervise the packing, moving, and unpacking of approximately _____ volumes of books to the new library building for a total cost of $_____.

_____ Storage and Transfer, Inc. agrees to furnish the following services and equipment in performing this move:

1. To furnish 2 vans, 2 drivers, and 2 supervisors for two eight-hour weekdays.
2. To furnish 50 four-wheel dollies, 600 tote boxes, labels and tape.
3. To furnish masonite or plywood for covering carpeting in the new building.
4. To advise and assist the library staff in developing a labeling and numbering system.
5. To supervise packers, unpackers, loaders and unloaders, provided by _____ Library, and to recommend manpower needs to accomplish this move in two days.
6. To furnish _____ Library with certificates of workmen's compensation and liability insurance.

_____ Library agrees to provide the following services in conjunction with these moves:

1. To properly number and mark all shelves so that books can be packed and placed in proper order.
2. To provide the necessary manpower to pack, unpack, load, and unload all books.
3. To release _____ Storage and Transfer, Inc. from any liability for loss or damage caused by the manpower

provided by _____ Library and for any injury to this manpower unless caused by the negligence of _____ Storage and Transfer, Inc. or its employees.

4. To provide a minimum of two weeks' notice for the dates of these moves.
5. To remove one window in the present library for installation of ramp for moving.

Accepted this _____ day of _____, 19__.

_____ Library   _____ Storage and Transfer, Inc.

By: _____   By: _____

LIST OF MOVERS

Below is a list of companies with experience in moving libraries which can be found in a search through classified section of the professional periodical literature. The information provided is from the companies themselves and should, in no way, be considered an endorsement of their services.

American Library Consultants Corp.
93 Fordham St.
Williston Park,
New York 11596
(516) 423-1225.

Integration and segregation of collections; supervision and move consultation; equipment rental; vacuuming and hand dusting; shelf reading; all shelving needs; fumigation of collections; furniture and stack layouts; long distance moving of collections; storage of collections (nationwide); preparation of move specifications; library furniture and stack relocation; building protection for moves; color coding, tagging, and labeling of collections; insertion of book theft detectors.

Apollo Moving Specialists
3300 Winpark Drive
Minneapolis,
Minnesota 55427
(800) 328-4815
From Minnesota call: (612) 544-5852

Agent for North American Van Lines

Previous moves include: U. of North Carolina at Chapel Hill;
Louisiana State University; U. of Minnesota; Hamline University of
Law; Duluth Public Library; York County Library, Rock Hill, SC;
Legislative reference Library, St. Paul, MN; Mayo Clinic; Chester
County Library, Chester, SC.

Fisher & Brother/N.J. Inc.
550 Myrtle Ave.
Boonton,
New Jersey 07005
(201) 334-0500

Specialists: New Jersey, New York and Philadelphia Metropolitan
Areas. Provide consulting, bid specs, steel work, specialized
equipment and actual moving services.

Hallett Movers:
The Only Mover You Need to Know
7535 W. 59th St.
Summit,
Illinois 60501
(800) 645-MOVE (6683)

Previous moves include: the Newberry Library, John Crerar Library
and UTEP.

Lewis & Michael, Inc.
1827 Woodman Drive
Dayton,
Ohio 45420
(513) 252-6683

Some of the libraries Lewis & Michael/Security Storage has moved: University of Cincinnati; Wright State University, Dayton; U.S. Court of Appeals Library, Cincinnati; Kalamazoo Public Library; Terra Tech Library, Freemont, Ohio; FBI Library, Cincinnati; Mt. St. Mary Library, Cincinnati.

Lewis & Michael Moving & Storage Co.
Irene Lane, General Manager
264 Centab Drive
Columbus,
Ohio 43202
(614) 258-9531

The Library Co-op, Inc.
Gloria Dinerman, President
3840 Park Ave.
Edison,
New Jersey 08820
(201) 906-1777
(212) 688-4534

Consulting services for all libraries
OCLC Input. Seminars. Publicity Writing. Editing. Moves. Inventory.

George McClain
4214 Longshore Ave.
Philadelphia,
Pennsylvania 19135
(215) 331-4428

Save thousands on that "Big Move." Experience in all collections:
Municipal. University. Archives. Law. Medical. Church. Private.
Since 1952, 50+ Libraries.

National Library Relocations, Inc.
71 S. Mall Drive
Commack,
New York 11725
(516) 543-2821

Consultation, budget figures, spec writing, shelving work and
equipment rental. Complete or partial collections. Merging,
segregation and shelf-to-shelf moves.

Security Storage Co.
706 Oak Street
Cincinnati,
Ohio 45206
(513) 961-2700
(an affiliate of Lewis & Michael)

Woodworth Storage and Transfer Company
1865 N. Kenmore
South Bend, Indiana
(219) 233-1111

Representative of Allied Van Lines

Previous moves include: Cushwa-Leighton Library, St. Mary's College, Notre Dame, IN; Bethel College Library, Mishawaka, IN.

SUGGESTIONS FOR FURTHER READING

CLEANING

Banks, Joyce M. *Guidelines for Preventive Conservation* Ottawa: Committee on Conservation/Preservation of Library Materials, 1981.

Bohem, Hilda. "Regional Conservation Services: What Can We Do Ourselves? (LJ Series on Preservation No. 5)" *Library Journal* 104 (1979): 1428-1431.

Swartzell, Ann. "Preservation" *RTSD Newsletter* 10 No. 7 (1985): 88-90.

DEACIDIFICATION

Banks, Joyce M. "Mass Deacidification at the National Library of Canada." *Conservation Administration News* #20 (January 1985).

Bohem, Hilda. "Regional Conservation Services: What Can We Do Ourselves? (LJ Series on Preservation No. 5)" *Library Journal* 104 (1979): 1428-1431.

Chepesiuk, Ron. "On Assignment: Preservation the Wei T'o Way" *Wilson Library Bulletin* 60 no. 10 (June 1986): 47-49+.

Harris, Carolyn. "Mass Deacidification: Science to the Rescue?" *Library Journal*104 (July 1979): 1423-7. Erratum: *Library Journal* 104 (November 1, 1979): 2250.

Nelson, Dale. "Deacidification at LC," *Wilson Library Bulletin* 59 (November 1984): 194-195.

-----. "Deacidification Priorities," *Wilson Library Bulletin* 59 (April 1985): 535.

Nyren, Karl. "The DEZ Process and the Library of Congress" *Library Journal* 111 no. 15 (September 15, 1986): 33-35.

-----. Demolition Team Knocks Out LC Deacidification Plant: NASA Acts to Remove Danger Seen After Two Accidents Involving Library of Congress DEZ Process" *Library Journal* 111 (April 1, 1986): 12-13.

Smith, Richard D. "Mass Deacidification Cost Comparisons," *College and Research Libraries News* 46 no. 3 (March 1985): 122-123.

-----. "Mass Deacidification: The Wei T'o Understanding" *College and Research Libraries News* 48 (January 1987): 2-10.

-----. "Mass Deacidification: The Wei T'o Way," *College and Research Libraries News* 45 no. 11 (December 1984): 588-593.

Sparks, Peter G. and Richard D. Smith. "Deacidification Dialogue," *College and Research Libraries News* No. 1 (January 1985): 9-11.

Wei T'o Associates, Inc. "Answers to Frequent Questions Regarding the Wei T'o Nonaqueous Book Deacidification System." Matteson, IL: Wei T'o Associates, June 16, 1986.

-----. "Using Wei T'o Deacidification Sprays and Solutions: Questions and Answers." Matteson, IL: Wei T'o Associates, June 15, 1984.

THE DEDICATION CEREMONY

Galbraith, Betty. "Planning for a Grand Opening" *Sourdough* 15 (January 1978): 20-21.

FUMIGATION

Carruthers, Ralph Herbert and Harry B. Weiss *Insect Pests of Books; An Annotated Bibliography to 1935* New York: New York Public Library, 1936.

Davis, Mary. "Preservation Using Pesticides: Some Words of Caution," *Wilson Library Bulletin* 59 (February 1985): 386-388+.

Hickin, Norman. *Bookworms: The Insect Pests of Books* Peoria, IL: Spoon River Press, 1985.

Nesheim, K. "The Yale Non-toxic Method of Eradicating Book-eating Insects by Deep Freezing." *Restaurator* 6 nos. 3-4 (1984): 147-164.

Smith, Richard D., "Fumigation Dilemma: More Overkill or Common Sense," *New Library Scene* 3 (December, 1984): 1,5-6.

MOVING LIBRARY COLLECTIONS

Allardyce, A. "Walkie-talkie in the Stacks" *NCL Occ. Newsletter* 7 (August 1966: 6.

Alley, Brian. "Carpeting the Stacks" *College and Research Libraries News* 47 no. 8 (September 1986): 517.

-----. "Moving Steel Stacks with a Special Dolly" *Library Acquisitions* 6 no. 3 (1982): 253-257.

-----. "A Utility Book Truck Designed for Moving Library Collections." *Library Acquisitions: Practice and Theory* 3 (1979): 33-37.

Ames, Mark. "How to Move a Library in One Easy Lesson, or Everything You Always Wanted to Know about Moving a Library but Were Afraid to Ask" *Michigan Librarian* 39 (Autumn 1973): 9-10.

Amodeo, Anthony J. "Helpful Hints for Moving or Shifting Collections," *College & Research Libraries News* 44 No. 3 (March, 1983): 82-83. Discussion: No. 5 (May 1983): 153; No. 6 (June 1983): 182; No. 7 (July 1983): 232.

Ansell, E. "The Move of the Cambridge University Library." *Library Association Record* 2 (March 1935): 92-96.

Baldwin, Leslie. "How to Move a Library," *New Library World* 83 (April 1982): 57-58.

Bauer, Harry C. "Moving Day," *Library Journal* 79 (Dec 15, 1954): 2384-2386.

Blaustein, Albert P. and Jessie L. Matthews. "Space for a Periodical Collection." *Law Library Journal* 60 (May 1967): 147-161.

Broaddus, Billie and Alice Hurlebaus. "Planning and Implementing a Major Journal Shift in a Health Sciences Library" *Bulletin of the Medical Library Association* 69 (October 1981): 395-396.

Brogan, Linda L. and Carolyn E. Lipscomb. "Moving the Collections of an Academic Health Sciences Library," *Bulletin of the Medical Library Association* 70 No. 4 (October 1982): 374-379.

Buckingham, A. J. "21 Miles of Books" Reprinted from *Reader: Chicago's Free Weekly* 11 no. 35 (June 11, 1982).

Chappell, D. LaMont. "Operation Move" *Utah Libraries* 7 (Spring 1964): 7-8+.

Checklist to Complete Orders for Terminals and Workstations Dublin, Ohio: OCLC, 1986.

Clifton, Mrs. A. "Moving JPL's Serials and Newspaper Collection Into a New Stack." *South African Librarian* 39 (July 1971): 56-59.

Daehn, Ralph M. "The Measurement and Projection of Shelf Space," *Collection Management* 4 (Winter 1982): 25-39.

"'Don't Return Books,' Says Moving Library Director," *American Libraries* 7 No. 9 (October 1976): 563.

Drake, Miriam A. "Forecasting Academic Library Growth" *College and Research Libraries* 37 (January 1976): 53-59.

Ducas, Ada M. "The Planning, Implementation and Moving of a Journal Collection in a Hospital Library" *Argus* 14 (September 1985): 75-79.

Fagan, George V. "Moving the Air Force Academy Library" *Mountain-Plains Library Quarterly* 3 (Winter 1959): 13-14.

Faller, Martha Lewkus, "Collection Shifting...From Crowding to User Comfort," *New Library Scene* 3 (August 1984): 9-10+.

Feret, Barbara L. "Moving the Library at Dutchess Community College," *ALA Bulletin* 61 (January 1967): 68-71.

Fitch, H. Glen. "Moving the Hillsdale College Library" *Michigan Librarian* 17 (October 1951): 7-8.

Fraley, Ruth A. and Carol Lee Anderson. *Library Space Planning: How to Assess, Allocate, and Reorganize Collections, Resources, and Physical Facilities* New York: Neal Schuman, 1985.

Gribbin, John H. "Tulane Library Moves Across the Street" *Louisiana Library Association Bulletin* 32 (Spring 1969): 26-30.

Hamilton, Patricia and Pam Hindman. "Moving a Public Library Collection" *Public Libraries* 26 (Spring 1987): 4-7.

Hammer, Donald P. "Operation Book Shift," *College and Research Libraries* 21 (September 1960): 393-394.

Hardkopf, Jewel. "A Major Book Move: Brooklyn Public Library Applies the Principles of Industrial Engineering and Moves a Half Million Books With Speed; The Time Study," *Library Journal* 80 (November 1, 1955): 2417-2419.

Hawthorne, Gladys S. "Library Moving Made Easy" *ALA Bulletin* 57 (July 1963): 671.

Hlavac, R. W. "Removal of the University of Otago Library" *New Zealand Libraries* 28 (May 1965): 73-82.

"How the Books Were Moved" *Yale University Library Gazette* 5 (October 1930): 30-34.

Hubbard, William J. *Stack Management: A Practical Guide to Shelving and Maintaining Library Collections* Chicago: American Library Association, 1981.

Ifidon, Sam E. "Moving an Academic Library," *Journal of Academic Librarianship* 4 (January 1979): 434-437.

Jesse, William Herman "Moving Books," *Library Quarterly* 11 (July 1941): 328-333.

Johnson, Nancy P. "Rearranging a Law Library: A Case Study," *Law Library Journal* 73 (winter 1980): 129-133.

Jones, Arthur and M. Barry King. "The Effect of Re-siting a Library" *Journal of Librarianship* 11 no. 3 (July 1979): 215-231.

Kelly, Robert Q. "Moving Your Law Library" *Law Library Journal* 51 (February 1958): 34-36.

Kephart, John Edgar. *Moving a Library* (Occasional papers, no. 21) Urbana: University of Illinois Library School, May 1951.

-----. *Moving a Library* (Occasional papers, no. 30--an expansion of no. 21.) Urbana: University of Illinois Library School, October, 1952.

-----. "Moving of Libraries," in *Encyclopedia of Library and Information Science.* (New York: Marcel Dekker, Inc., c1976.) Vol. 18:283-286.

Kinney, Lisa. "Albany Co. Library on the Move" *Wyoming Library Roundup* 37 (Fall 1981): 1-3.

Kurkul, Donna Lee. "The Planning, Implementation and Movement of an Academic Library Collection." *College and Research Libraries* 44 No. 4 (July, 1983): 220-234. Discussion 44 (November 1983): 486-487.

Kurth, William. H. & Roy W. Grim. *Moving a Library* (New York: Scarecrow Press, 1966.)

Leary, Margaret A. "The Move of the University of Michigan Law Library." *Law Library Journal* 75 (Spring 1982): 308-313.

Lee, Lionel James. "Always so Much to Move," *Library Journal* 75 (April 1, 1950): 534-537.

"Library Moves [1979 Texas Library Association Conference Program]." *Texas Library Journal* 55 (Spring 1979): 37.

Long, Frances G. and Margaret R. Meyer. "Library on the Move: *Wilson Library Bulletin* 28 (May 1954): 793-795.

Lukasiewicz, Barbara and Marcia Preston. "University of Michigan-Dearborn Library: A Moving Experience" (unpublished article) Dearborn, MI: University of Michigan - Dearborn Library, 198?.

Lumb, Audrey E. "Moving an Academic Library: A Case Study." *Journal of Librarianship* 4 No. 4 (October 1972): 253-271.

Metcalf, Keyes DeWitt; Philip D. Leighton; and David C. Weber *Planning Academic and Research Library Buildings* 2nd ed. Chicago: American Library Association, 1986.

Moran, Robert F. Jr. "Moving a Large Library," *Special Libraries* 63 No. 4 (April 1972): 163-171.

Peacock, P. G. "Measuring a Library" *Aslib Proceedings* 35 (March 1983): 152-155.

"Princeton University Moves into its New Building" *Library Journal* 73 (September 1, 1948): 1210-1213.

Roberts, Matt T. "Some Ideas on Moving a Book Collection," *College and Research Libraries* 27 (March 1966): 103-108.

Segesta, James. "Pulling the Rug Out From Under the Stacks." *College and Research Libraries News* 47 No. 7 (July/August 1986): 441-444.

Sell, Violet G. "Moving can be Fun!" *Wilson Library Bulletin* 28 (May 1954): 792, 795.

Shercliff, W. H. "Removing a College of Education Library: A Case Study of the Removal of 70,000 Books" *Education Libraries Bulletin* 17 (Summer 1974): 15-27.

Spyers-Duran, Peter. *Moving Library Materials* Rev. ed. Chicago: American Library Association, 1965.

Stebbins, Howard L. "Moving Day," *Wilson Library Bulletin* 15 (May 1941): 425.

Stickney, Edith P. and Janet Larsen Meinhold. "Operation Big Switch" *Wilson Library Bulletin* 30 (November 1955): 253-255.

Stokes, Katharine M. and Margaret F. Knoll. "Moving the Pennsylvania State College Library," *Wilson Library Bulletin* 16 (November 1941): 230-238.

User's Guide to M300 Workstation Installation Dublin, Ohio: OCLC, August, 1985.

Vollmar, Rev. E. R. "Operation Beer Case," *Library Journal* 85 (Jan. 1, 1960): 46-48.

Waldron, Helen J. "How to Move Documents" *Special Libraries* 49 (July 1958): 266-267.

Waters, David H. "Problems of Merging Libraries." *Australian Academic and Research Libraries* 12 (September 1981): 167-173.

Weaver-Meyers, Pat and Dale Francis Wasowski. "A Committee Approach to Moving a Library: Planning, Personnel, and Stress," *Journal of Library Administration* 5 No. 4 (Winter 1984): 21-32.

Wittenborg, Karen and John F. Camp. *Shelf Space Projection Survey* n.p.: SUNY Council of Head Librarians, 1977.

Woodward, W. B. "Laughing All the Way to the Stacks," *Library Association Record* 79 (July 1977): 365.

Wright, Shirley Louise. "N. J. Library Lightens Move," *Library Journal* 80 (August 1955): 1662-1663.

WEEDING

Bess, E. D. and E. Love. "Faculty Participation in an Evaluation Review of Low Use Journals" *Bulletin of the Medical Library Association* 66 (October 1978): 461-463.

Engeldinger, Eugene A. "Weeding of Academic Library Reference Collections: A Survey of Current Practice" *RQ* (Spring 1986): 366-371.

Lawrence, Gary S. "A Cost Model for Storage and Weeding Programs," *College and Research Libraries* 42 (March 1981): 139-147.

Slote, Stanley J. *Weeding Library Collections--II* 2nd rev. ed. Littleton, Colo: Libraries Unlimited, 1982.

INDEX

DISCARD

DATE DUE

ILL 8/18/90			
GAYLORD			PRINTED IN U.S.A.